DID THE

RESURRECTION

HAPPEN . . . REALLY?

[A DIALOGUE ON LIFE, DEATH, AND HOPE]

COFFEE　　　　HOUSE

CHRONICLES

DID THE

RESURRECTION

HAPPEN . . . REALLY?

JOSH MCDOWELL
AND DAVE STERRETT

MOODY PUBLISHERS
CHICAGO

All Scripture quotations, unless otherwise indicated, are taken from the *Holy Bible, New International Version*®, NIV®. Copyright ©1973, 1978, 1984 by Biblica, Inc.™ Used by permission of Zondervan. All rights reserved worldwide.

All Scripture quotations marked NASB are taken from the *New American Standard Bible*®, Copyright © 1960, 1962, 1963, 1968, 1971, 1972, 1973, 1975, 1977, 1995 by The Lockman Foundation. Used by permission. (www.Lockman.org)

All Scripture quotations marked NLT are taken from the *Holy Bible, New Living Translation*, copyright © 1996, 2004. Used by permission of Tyndale House Publishers, Inc., Wheaton, Illinois 60189, U.S.A. All rights reserved.

All Scripture quotations marked ESV are taken from *The Holy Bible, English Standard Version*. Copyright © 2000, 2001 by Crossway Bibles, a division of Good News Publishers. Used by permission. All rights reserved.

All Scripture quotations marked NKJV are taken from the *New King James Version*. Copyright © 1982 by Thomas Nelson, Inc. Used by permission. All rights reserved.

All Scripture quotations marked KJV are taken from the King James Version.

Edited by Paul Santhouse	Cover design: Faceout Studio
Interior design: Ragont Design	Cover images: Getty #85525885, #6032134
Sterrett Photo: Katherine Robertson	McDowell Photo: Barbara Gannon

Library of Congress Cataloging-in-Publication Data

McDowell, Josh.
    Did the resurrection happen—really? : a dialogue on life, death, and hope / Josh McDowell and Dave Sterrett.
      p. cm. -- (The coffeehouse chronicles ; 3)
    Includes bibliographical references.
    ISBN 978-0-8024-8768-1
    1. Jesus Christ—Resurrection. 2. Jesus Christ--Crucifixion. 3. Jesus Christ—Historicity. I. Sterrett, Dave. II. Title.
    BT482.M325 2011
    232'.5—dc22
                                      2010042289

This is a work of fiction. Names, characters, places, and incidents either are the product of the authors' imagination or are used fictitiously, and any resemblance to actual persons, living or dead, businesses, companies, events, or locales is entirely coincidental.

All websites and phone numbers listed herein are accurate at the time of publication, but may change in the future or cease to exist. The listing of website references and resources does not imply publisher endorsement of the site's entire contents. Groups and organizations are listed for informational purposes, and listing does not imply publisher endorsement of their activities.

We hope you enjoy this book from Moody Publishers. Our goal is to provide high-quality, thought-provoking books and products that connect truth to your real needs and challenges. For more information on other books and products written and produced from a biblical perspective, go to www.moodypublishers.com or write to:

Moody Publishers
820 N. LaSalle Boulevard
Chicago, IL 60610

1 3 5 7 9 10 8 6 4 2

Printed in the United States of America

To

Dr. Robert Saucy,
my professor and mentor for three years.
Who always challenged me to love Jesus,
study the Scriptures, and pursue Truth.
—Josh

To

Dr. Gary Habermas,
my professor of Theology.
—Dave

CONTENTS

One

TENSION ON CAMPUS

TENSION ON CAMPUS was thick. The administrators of Opal University could not remember a more volatile season. Factions among the student body were growing militant, and violence seemed a real possibility.

Politics and social issues were always volatile topics among students, but strained relations had boiled over when one of the Opal instructors presented a strong case for the historical Christ during a debate with two visiting scholars—an atheist and an agnostic. The ensuing weeks had seen nonstop confrontations, sometimes ugly, between religious and atheist groups on campus.

Jamal Washington, the instructor who presented the historical Christ at the debate, was a doctoral student who taught several undergraduate courses in the school of religion. He was also thought to be responsible for the faith conversions of *emeritus* religion professor, Dr. William Peterson, and several students from the atheist club.

One month after the debate, Dr. Peterson delivered a stirring lecture on the deity of Christ, and even more students came to believe that Jesus was the Son of God. It was after Dr. Peterson's lecture that Jamal received his first piece of hate mail.

The unsigned letter was on his office floor one morning, evidently slipped under the door. Jamal didn't seem too worried about it. He viewed the controversy as harmless "hot air" stirred up by a few opinionated student leaders. While the atheist club members certainly didn't agree with Washington and Peterson, they weren't hostile.

Brett, an agnostic and former leader in the atheist club, was beginning to question his own skepticism. His family, well educated and academic, had a history of investigating new ideas before embracing them, and Brett was taking his time with this Jesus thing. No one would ever accuse Brett of an emotional conversion to anything—especially religious faith.

Earlier in the week, at Nick's invitation, Brett had attended a class taught by Dr. Peterson. Though *emeritus*,

Dr. Peterson frequently filled in for his former colleagues in the religion department. The topic of Jesus' resurrection had come up in class, and Brett decided to stop by the religion hall to ask Dr. Peterson a few questions. The resurrection was a key issue in his pursuit of truth.

Brett was within a block of the religion hall when he noticed students running from the building. *Must be a fire drill*, he thought. But something wasn't right. *Nobody runs during fire drills.* Then he heard screaming. Brett was a premed major and wired for action, and the screaming kicked him into response mode. "Gotta go!" he shouted as he flipped his phone closed, shoved it in his pocket, and took off at a run *toward* whatever was happening.

Students were pouring from the religion hall, screaming and running in every direction. As Brett approached, one girl stumbled and collapsed on the lawn not twenty feet in front of him. It actually looked like there was blood all over her T-shirt. Brett crouched beside her. She was breathing in short gasps and seemed frantic to get back up.

"Where are you hurt?" Brett shouted amidst the chaos. "What happened?"

"I'm shot!" she screamed. "He's shooting everyone!"

Brett immediately grabbed his cell phone, dialed 9-1-1, and with a shaky voice yelled for help. The call took under a minute, and then he lifted the girl in his arms and, as fast as he could, moved her to a safe place across the street. She was crying hysterically.

"Where are you hurt?"

"My shoulder!" She seemed to be slipping into shock.

Now there were sirens everywhere and police cars were arriving from all directions. Police officers poured out and ran toward the building. It was all happening so fast it seemed like a dream . . . a bad dream that didn't make any sense.

The girl in Brett's lap passed out.

Two

GRIEVING

SLOWLY, THE STORY unfolded. Dr. Peterson and his wife, Susan, clung to each other and sobbed as they watched the nonstop news coverage, now on every channel. Nine students had died in a shooting at the school of religion . . . including Jamal Washington, Nick Ridley, and the shooter, who eventually turned the gun on himself. Dr. Peterson was wracked with grief *and* guilt. He couldn't stop berating himself for not seeing this coming. Why had he not pressed the administration or police to investigate all the hate literature and threats?

"Bill, don't put this guilt on yourself. There is nothing more you could have done to stop it. You reported every one of those notes to the authorities," said Susan Peterson as she tried to console her husband.

So far, the news coverage had revealed that the shooter was a student. Like so many similar campus killers, he was a troubled young man. A loner with few friends. His roommate said in an interview, "He never even talked to *me*. We sometimes invited him to hang out with us, but he always said 'no' and acted awkward around us. We had no idea he was planning to kill anyone. We just thought he was weird."

Another student, a member of the atheist club, commented that he had seen the suspected shooter attend several of the atheists' meetings. "He rarely spoke up, but when he did he always seemed angry about the Christians. Definite anger issues."

"Bill," Susan said as she turned back to the TV coverage, "this student being interviewed looks familiar."

"Yes, you're right," Bill replied. "That's Brett. Nick brought him over here after my lecture. In fact, I was supposed to meet with him this morning."

"Okay, I remember. Was he the one with the motorcycle?"

"That's him. A premed major, and a very bright boy."

The reporter turned to face the camera and said, "We're talking with Brett Wilson, a senior at Opal University, who was on his way to meet with a religion professor when he saw a young coed, covered in blood, running out of the religion building. Brett, tell us again what happened."

"Well, students were pouring from the building, and one of them, a young woman, collapsed in front of me as I approached the front doors. I noticed she had blood all over her shoulder, so I called 9-1-1 and within minutes the police arrived."

"You also mentioned—before we went on the air—that you had indeed met the suspected killer several months ago."

"That's right. I don't remember his name, but he showed up a few times at the atheist club. He didn't fit in very well and seemed awkward in a group setting. He said things that made people uncomfortable. But he sure was intelligent. I remember arguing with him at one point."

"Why did you argue with him?" the reporter asked.

"Like I mentioned earlier, he was pretty angry most of the time. He came to one of our meetings saying that, if there's no God, there's no right or wrong. Since we're merely the result of a deterministic evolutionary process, we should get rid of all religion, people with genetic defects, and inferior races. That's what we argued about, and we asked him not to come back since we don't put up with racism in the club. We never saw him again after that."

"Why didn't you report this?" asked the reporter.

"Honestly, none of us took him seriously. We figured he was taking freshman philosophy and trying it out on our group. We never assumed he was for real about getting rid of people. You meet a lot of racists on campus, and mostly they don't come back once they realize we don't share their views. We had no idea this guy was serious, and until yesterday none of us knew Mr. Washington had received death threats."

As the Petersons continued watching, they cried and prayed that despite the horror, God would somehow be glorified in this senseless tragedy. They prayed for Nick's parents, for Jamal's family, and for all the others impacted by the event. Especially Nick and Jamal's close friends, Jessica, Mina, Andrea, and Brett.

Three

VALENTINE'S DAY

A DOZEN WOMEN from the campus ministry sat around the table laughing. It was February 14, and they were enjoying dessert at the Cheesecake Factory. Andrea was telling hilarious stories, and the new girls appeared to be fitting in well. While the girls laughed, Jessica noticed roses on the table of a nearby young couple. She had been thinking about Nick all day and missed him terribly. Almost three months had passed since he was taken, and even though she believed God allowed the tragedy, she was still hurting.

As the conversation drifted down the table, Andrea leaned over and said, "I feel for you, Jessica. I know that today is very hard for you."

"Thanks, Andrea. I'm sorry I was zoning out. Somehow, even in the company of my very best friends, I still feel lonely."

"No, you're fine. Nick was wonderful and courageous, and I know you miss him."

The news media had reported that Nick actually died trying to protect Jamal. Remarkably, the networks had cited Jesus' words, "Greater love has no one than this, than to lay down one's life for his friends,"[1] in describing Nick's heroic action. The shooting catalyzed many of the Christians to be bold in demonstrating and explaining their faith, and the Christian campus ministries had doubled in attendance.

Several of the girls had heard Jessica and Andrea talking, and now the whole group was quietly watching them. Fighting tears, Jessica responded, "I'm so thankful for all you girls. I love you all and there's nowhere I'd rather be than right here with you."

"We love you too, Jessica, and one day we'll all get to see Nick and Jamal again," Andrea said.

What? How do we know that? Lauren thought to herself as Andrea comforted Jessica. Lauren, a medical student, had met this group of girls through her friendships with Andrea and Brett on the atheist club. Though all three had since left the club, she remained agnostic and didn't share the others' convictions about heaven.

Each Wednesday night the campus ministry leaders met for coffee and discussion at the Caruth Haven Coffeehouse. Though their meetings were *very* difficult in the weeks following the shooting, they kept meeting, and now they'd regained their easy rhythm. Jessica especially looked forward to their time, despite missing Nick.

When they'd all settled in the Wednesday after Valentine's Day, Lauren was the first to speak. "Okay, you all know I have a lot of spiritual questions. Here's my first, and I apologize for the insensitivity of it, but I can't stop wondering about heaven. You've mentioned it often since the ... um ... since last fall when ..."

"Since the shooting," said Andrea.

Lauren nodded, glancing at Jessica and Mina. "Why are you so sure about the idea of heaven, and what do you picture when you say it?"

Jessica replied first. "Lauren, Jesus often spoke of heaven. One of my favorite passages is in John, chapter fourteen, where Jesus told His disciples, 'In my Father's house are many rooms. If it were not so, would I have told you that I go to prepare a place for you? And if I go and prepare a place for you, I will come again and will take you to myself, that where I am you may be also.'[2] I memorized that verse because it reminds me that Jesus wants to spend eternity with us. There's another passage that I love from the book of Revelation, but I don't have it memorized. I have it on my phone. Hold on a second."

Lauren just listened even though she inwardly disagreed. *I really shouldn't break it to her, but many other religions refer to the afterlife. Christianity isn't unique in making heaven claims.*

Jessica found her verse. "In the book of Revelation, God gave John a vision of heaven. Here's how John described it:"

And I heard a loud voice from the throne saying, "Behold, the dwelling place of God is with man. He will dwell with them, and they will be his people, and God himself will be with them as their God. He will wipe away every tear from their eyes, and death shall be no more, neither shall there be mourning, nor crying, nor pain anymore, for the former things have passed away.[3]

Amy, another agnostic who came with Lauren, spoke up next. "Okay, does this mean our friends who died are in heaven right now? Or is that in the future?"

Jessica responded, "I think they're in heaven right now, but maybe Mina has some insight here."

Mina, a law student at Opal, spoke with more confidence than Jessica. "That's a good question, Amy. Actually, it's both. We know God will create a new heaven and new earth because the Bible says so in 2 Peter and Revelation. I also believe our friends are in a real place called heaven right now because there's biblical evidence for this as well. Jesus told the thief on the cross, 'Today you will be with me in Paradise.'[4] And Paul wrote to the church at Corinth that he 'would prefer to be away from the body and at home with the Lord.'"[5]

Four

JESUS TALKS ABOUT HEAVEN

ANDREA JUMPED into the conversation. "I just read that story Jesus told about the rich man and Lazarus. He describes both men dying and going to . . . well, Lazarus goes right to heaven."

"I'm not familiar with that one," said Lauren. "Tell me more."

"Okay, give me a minute. Let me see if I have my Bible in my purse . . . nope. I don't have a Bible on me. Jess, can you read that story? It's in Luke sixteen."

"Sure." Jess was still learning her way around the Bible, so it took her a few moments. "Okay, this is sort of long, so hang with me."

Jesus said, "There was a certain rich man who was splendidly clothed in purple and fine linen and who lived each day in luxury. At his gate lay a poor man named Lazarus who was covered with sores. As Lazarus lay there longing for scraps from the rich man's table, the dogs would come and lick his open sores.

"Finally, the poor man died and was carried by the angels to be with Abraham. The rich man also died and was buried, and his soul went to the place of the dead. There, in torment, he saw Abraham in the far distance with Lazarus at his side.

"The rich man shouted, 'Father Abraham, have some pity! Send Lazarus over here to dip the tip of his finger in water and cool my tongue. I am in anguish in these flames.'

"But Abraham said to him, 'Son, remember that during your lifetime you had everything you wanted, and Lazarus had nothing. So now he is here being comforted, and you are in anguish. And besides, there is a great chasm separating us. No one can cross over to you from here, and no one can cross over to us from there.'

"Then the rich man said, 'Please, Father Abraham, at least send him to my father's home. For I have five brothers, and I want him to warn them so they don't end up in this place of torment.'

"But Abraham said, 'Moses and the prophets have

warned them. Your brothers can read what they wrote.'

"The rich man replied, 'No, Father Abraham! But if someone is sent to them from the dead, then they will repent of their sins and turn to God.'

"But Abraham said, 'If they won't listen to Moses and the prophets, they won't listen even if someone rises from the dead.'"[6]

As Jessica was reading, Andrea was watching Lauren tap her fingers and stare into space. *She doesn't seem to like that story very much.*

No one said anything when Jessica finished, so Mina spoke up. "Jessica was right when she said Jesus often spoke of heaven. Here's another one." She flipped her Bible to Luke and read, "But when you give a banquet, invite the poor, the crippled, the lame, the blind, and you will be blessed. Although they cannot repay you, you will be repaid at the resurrection of the righteous."[7]

Andrea interrupted. "What are you thinking, Lauren? I know you're holding back."

Lauren shot Andrea a look. "I really don't want to say anything that's going to offend or upset you guys. I know you miss Jamal and Nick, and I respect you for believing that you'll see them in heaven. It's not that I'm against believing in the idea of God and heaven, but the story you just read isn't that unique. Lots of philosophers and teachers spoke of the afterlife. It wasn't just Jesus. I don't mean to be rude, but seriously, what makes Jesus' teaching on the afterlife more believable than the teachings of Socrates, or Siddhartha Gautama, or Mohammed?"

"Because what Jesus said makes more sense," Andrea blurted.

"Maybe to you, but to a Buddhist or Muslim or someone else, maybe another view makes more sense. Why should we believe Jesus over them?"

"The resurrection," Mina shot back.

Lauren raised her eyebrows. *She'll be one good litigator when she's done with law school.*

"What's that supposed to mean?" asked Andrea. "How does the resurrection make Jesus different?"

"Jesus didn't just talk about the afterlife. He *demonstrated* it."

"How so, Mina?" Lauren asked.

"Well, until the time of Christ, some of the Jews believed that in the end, the bones would be resurrected back to life. But for many of them it was speculation with no proof. Then Jesus comes on the scene saying things like, 'There will be a resurrection of the body' and 'I am the resurrection and the life. He who believes in me will live, even though he dies; and whoever lives and believes in me will never die.'[8] Then Jesus started calling for people to believe in Him to receive the full promises of the resurrection. Next, He told His disciples that He was going to be delivered into the hands of sinful men, be crucified, and on the third day be raised again.[9] Jesus' predictive words would be proven as He later fulfilled these details and physically rose again from the dead. Jesus also told His followers, 'Because I live, you also will live.'"[10]

Lauren had heard enough. She was frustrated by all these claims of Jesus' resurrection, yet wasn't sure how to contradict them. She also wanted to avoid another religious argument where she was always getting outsmarted. *Maybe God does exist, but this Jesus stuff seems far-fetched and fanatical to me,* Lauren thought. *So how do I work my way out of this?*

"Girls, I didn't mean to get us into a religious argument tonight. I know your Christian faith is comforting to you, but I really don't think you can know that Jesus' resurrection is true. I mean, even if I were a Christian I don't think I could believe He literally came back from the dead. He had some nice sayings, and I know Christianity is all about people having good and positive thoughts, loving each other without judging, and striving for social justice, but why the big deal about a resurrection?"

Lauren frowned, and then continued. "You know, even the pastor in my home church didn't believe it was literal. He used to say that Christ arises in the hearts of those who believe. That always made good sense to my parents, and I don't see what's wrong with it."

This time, Jessica spoke up. "Lauren, if you ever decide to become a Christian, you'll need to believe in the historical resurrection of Christ. It's the foundation of Christianity. The apostle Paul said, 'If Christ has not been raised, your faith is futile; you are still in your sins.'[11] Without the resurrection, Christianity doesn't work. Jesus died to pay for the sin of the world. If He had been guilty of sin Himself, He would not have come back to life since the penalty for sin is death. The fact that He came back to life proves He was sinless, and that means His death was a legitimate payment for my sin. Everyone's sin. That's why Paul said we are still in our sins if Christ didn't rise from the dead. It would have meant His payment was not accepted by God. I know this will sound rude, but I have to tell you this. A person who denies the bodily resurrection of Jesus Christ is not a true Christian."

How judgmental is that!? Who is she to decide who is a real Christian or not? "Well, thanks for giving us your opinion, Jessica," said Lauren. "It's a little intolerant, but I know you're still hurting. I also know Brett and Scott are more interested in this historical Christ stuff than I am. Maybe we should save all this till the next time they join us."

"That's a good idea," said Mina. "Besides, I need to get back and hit the books. Major exam tomorrow."

Five

WHY DID JESUS HAVE TO DIE?

"HOW WAS LAST NIGHT?" asked Brett. He'd spotted Lauren walking to a class and hurried to catch up with her.

"It was weird. I love those girls, and I know they care about me, but they have answers for *everything*," said Lauren.

"Maybe they believe it."

Lauren looked at him. "What's that supposed to mean?"

 "Remember that time we were with Jason and Regina, and they started making comments about health care? You had no trouble making your case that night. In fact, I don't think Regina has ever forgiven you!"

They laughed, recalling the awkward scene. "And your point is?" said Lauren.

"Just that those girls care about their faith. They've looked into it and they're always studying to discover what's true."

Lauren stopped in the middle of the sidewalk. "Brett, do you have something to tell me?"

"No, I'm just saying don't get bent out of shape about all their answers. They care about what they believe and I respect them for that."

"I care about what I believe too," said Lauren. "That's why I don't believe in myths and legends."

The following Wednesday evening, Andrea and Jessica showed up early and sat on the outside furniture. As they waited for their friends to arrive, they discussed school, the previous night's *I am Second* meeting, and how much they still missed Nick. They were praying for tonight's conversation when Lauren, Scott, Amy, and Brett arrived.

They talked for a while about the East Coast hurricane, the new receiver picked up by the Dallas Cowboys in a recent trade, and a professor fired from another university over his statements on morality. Then Brett turned the conversation toward their topic from last week.

"Andrea and Jessica, Lauren told me about your discussion last week on the resurrection. You both know I've always been an atheist, but recently I've become interested in the afterlife and the possibility of heaven. Could you tell me more about the relationship between the afterlife and Christ's physical resurrection? I've heard this mentioned by Christian philosophers but still don't get your point."

Jessica spoke first. "Jesus told His disciples that because He lived, they would also live, even though He also predicted their deaths. In other words, Jesus was promising eternal life. John recorded Jesus promising eternal life to His followers, but also in some of His final words, Jesus told Peter that he was going to be martyred. I wish Mina or Dr. Peterson were here to help explain it in an academic sense. From what I remember, there were some Jewish groups like the Pharisees who believed the human body would one day be raised, but Jesus didn't just teach about it. He actually demonstrated it and proved His claims by literally rising from the dead."

Lauren replied, "Why do you Christians believe that Jesus had to die? Why would a loving God resort to such cruelty?"

"The purpose of Christ's death was to restore our relationship to God," said Jessica. "All of us are born as sinners, and sinners cannot stand before God because He's holy. Sin is like dirt. If you're working in your garden and come inside all covered in mud and sweat, you can't go bear hug your sister who's trying on her wedding dress. You have to get cleaned up first. That's how it is with sin and God. Unfortunately, the only payment for sin is death, and only the death of a perfect person can pay for someone else's sin. Only something clean can cleanse something dirty."[12] Jessica paused, collecting her thoughts.

"Go on," said Brett.

"Well, the only person who was ever perfect was Jesus Christ. He was perfect because He was God's Son, not the son of a sinful man. So Jesus was the only person who could pay the price for someone else's sin. One of my favorite verses is John 3:16. It says, 'For God so loved the world that He gave His only begotten Son, that whoever believes in Him should not perish but have everlasting life.'"[13]

Brett jumped in, "Okay, Jessica, let me play devil's advocate. If God is all-powerful, why can't He just forgive everyone? I mean, if Scott does something evil to me, I can forgive him. Nobody has to be tortured or killed. If God is God and can do anything, why can't He just forgive us? Why did Jesus have to die?"

"Can I answer this one?" asked Andrea.

"Sure," Brett replied.

"I used to wonder the same thing. Here's the answer. God *can't* do everything. He can't do things that are contrary to His nature. Scripture says so."

"How's that?" said Scott. "I thought God was supposed to be able to do anything."

Andrea replied, "Think about it, Scott. The Bible says it's impossible for God to lie. Why? Because He is truth. It is impossible for God to do illogical actions, like make a 'married bachelor' or a 'square circle' or a 'stone so big He can't lift it.' God can't sin. He is a God of order and holiness and can't do anything contrary to His character or who He is."

"So, Andrea or Jessica, explain again how this connects with Jesus having to die," said Lauren.

"Sure," replied Jessica. "This is what I was trying to describe with the wedding dress example. God in His character is holy. That means He is separated completely from sin. His nature, or *character* as Andrea called it, is also *just* and *righteous*. For Him to let sin go unpunished would be unjust. However, God is also *love*. So He sent His Son, Jesus Christ, to be the perfect sacrifice to pay for sin. In the Old Testament, the priest would slaughter a perfect lamb and confess the sins of the people. Even though such a sacrifice was not adequate—animals can't pay for the sins of people—God allowed it to foreshadow something better to come. That 'something better' was Christ. Since the sacrifice had to be perfect, it had to be God, since only God is perfect. And since it had to be human in order to pay for the sin of humans, God had to take on human form. So Christ, who was fully God and existed with God from all eternity,[14] took on humanity and came to earth to die for us. He satisfied both the justice and holiness of God, and expressed God's love at the same time. That's why we can be forgiven."

"Beautiful explanation, Jessica. What she just described is called propitiation," said Mina as she pulled up a chair.

"Good to see you, Mina," said Lauren.

"Good to see you too—all of you!"

"Mina," said Brett. "We're talking about the death and resurrection of Christ, along with the implications of heaven. Logically, I have not been convinced that there is any connection. Maybe you can tell us why you believe the resurrection is so important?"

"Well, the resurrection of Jesus demonstrates His defeat of death. As Christians, we grieve over death but still have hope—the hope of eternal life. Brett, you know Jamal and I were close, right? He was probably my best guy friend ever. I cared about him deeply, and for the first two months following his death, I couldn't even concentrate on my studies. If it weren't for two of my professors giving me extensions, I'd be a semester behind right now. But once the sharp pain of missing him *right now* began to fade, I took heart in the fact that I will see him again because Jesus conquered death. There is life after death. Jesus proved it by His resurrection, and talked about it while on the earth. Jessica and Andrea, even though you also suffered loss at the shooting, would you agree that you have hope?"

"Yes," Jessica said, tearing up. "I had prayed that I would marry Nick and when we started dating again, I seriously thought he was *the one*. I'm still not fully over it, but the resurrection of Jesus gives me motivation to get out of bed every morning and live life to the fullest, even though I'm still sad and sometimes depressed."

"Well, I'm really glad that works for you," Lauren responded.

Andrea glared at her.

"What? I'm serious!"

"What you're saying is that even though 'it works' for Jessica, it's not objectively true. You are implying that her faith is false."

"Sorry," Lauren responded.

Amy cleared her throat and they all turned toward her. "Okay, I'm not as smart as Lauren or Brett, but I want to know why you think you have such hope."

Jessica smiled. "For me it's because Jesus is a personal God who came as a real man and understands suffering and death. When Nick died, I felt I suffered a deeper grief than anyone else could relate to, but I know now that wasn't true. God the Father knows what loss is like because He lost His Son. He can identify with me and has been my 'refuge and strength, a very present help in trouble.'[15] The most familiar of all the psalms makes the claim that we will not be alone in death. 'Even though I walk through the valley of the shadow of death, I fear no evil, for You are with me; Your rod and Your staff, they comfort me.'"[16]

Mina added, "Like Jessica, I grieved with the loss of Jamal and Nick and the other students when they were murdered three months ago. One of my favorite verses from Paul is from 1 Thessalonians where he says, 'But we do not want you to be uninformed, brothers, about those who are asleep, that you may not grieve as others do who have no hope.'[17] Paul wasn't saying that Christians don't grieve, but that our grieving isn't like those who have no hope in Christ and the afterlife."

Six

CAN I BE A CHRISTIAN WITHOUT BELIEVING IN THE RESURRECTION?

"OKAY, I HAVE A QUESTION for you all," Lauren said. "Last week I mentioned that I was open to the idea of believing in God, and that I could even see being a Christian without believing in the resurrection of Jesus. Then one of you said—I think it was you, Jessica—that you can't be a Christian without the resurrection. I felt it was kind of intolerant and said so. What I'd like to know is why not? Why can't I be a Christian without believing in the resurrection?"

Brett shook his head. "I know you emailed us about that, Lauren, but I didn't have any time to look into it this past week. Sorry about that."

"I found a book about it," said Scott, a doctoral student in history. "I discovered some atheists who have written on the subject and I also read some research by Dr. Gerd Lüdemann. Though he criticizes the miracles in the gospels, he seems to recognize the importance of the resurrection to Christianity."

Scott rummaged through his backpack as he talked. "Okay, here it is. Lüdemann writes, 'The resurrection of Jesus is the central point of the Christian religion. . . . Evidently everything quite simply depends on the event of the resurrection of Jesus.'"[18]

Mina looked at Scott and Lauren "We may disagree with Lüdemann about whether or not the resurrection happened, but he hit the nail on the head, regarding its importance."

Jessica glanced at Lauren. "Lauren, the reason I said what I did wasn't because I was being intolerant. I said what I did because after I became a Christian and began reading the New Testament, the *resurrection* seems to have been the focus of the church since its inception. The New Testament book of Acts, which tells the story of the beginning of the Christian church, illustrates this well. I underlined some verses that illustrate what I mean. Can I show them to you?"

"Sure. I actually brought my own Bible so I could check out some of the claims you guys have been making," Lauren responded.

Jessica opened her Bible. "In the first chapter of Acts, the eleven apostles were trying to decide on a replacement for Judas, who had hanged himself after Jesus' trial. One criterion for the selection of an apostle was that he 'must become a witness with us of His resurrection.'[19] Lauren, if you want to follow with me, go to the next chapter. Here, Peter gives his first sermon on the day of Pentecost. The keynote of his address was the death and resurrection of Christ. Would you like to read Acts 2:23–24?"

"Sure." Lauren found the page and read, "This Man, delivered over by the predetermined plan and foreknowledge of God, you nailed to a cross by the hands of godless men and put Him to death. But God raised Him up again, putting an end to the agony of death, since it was impossible for Him to be held in its power."[20]

Jessica continued, "Then, in Peter's second sermon he says, 'but put to death the Prince of life, the one whom God raised from the dead, *a fact to which* we are witnesses.'[21]

"Also, Lauren, on my Bible computer program, I discovered that Paul refers to the resurrection of Jesus fifty-three times in his letters. Most of these texts assert the primacy of the resurrection, the assurance it gives us, and the hope of our own future bodily resurrection. I made note of one passage in which Paul emphasized the centrality of the resurrection in his letter to the Thessalonians." Jessica turned to the passage and read, "For they themselves report about us what kind of a reception we had with you, and how you turned to God from idols to serve a living and true God, and to wait for His Son from heaven, *whom He raised from the dead*, that is Jesus, who rescues us from the wrath to come."[22]

"Okay, Jessica, I can kind of see why you think the resurrection is important to the Christian faith. And I'm amazed at how you know your Bible. But I always thought Christianity was centered more in the *teachings* of Jesus."

Andrea seemed eager to respond to this one. "The teachings of Christ are important, but the resurrection of Christ is central to the life of the church. I brought a book on this subject from N. T. Wright, a British scholar and expert on this subject." She opened and read from one of the books sitting on the table in front of her.

There is no form of early Christianity known to us— though there are some that have been invented by ingenious scholars—that does not affirm at its heart that after Jesus' shameful death God raised him to life again. Already by the time of Paul, our earliest written records, the resurrection of Jesus is not just a single detached article of faith. It is woven into the very structure of Christian life and thought.[23]

Andrea set the book down and opened another, in which she had several bookmarkers. "Let me read another conclusion found in the *Dictionary of the Apostolic Church*."

> Dr. F. Strauss, e.g., the most trenchant and remorseless of the church's critics in dealing with the Resurrection, acknowledges that it is the 'touchstone not of lives of Jesus only, but of Christianity itself,' that it 'touches all Christianity to the quick,' and is 'decisive for the whole view of Christianity' (*New Life of Jesus*, Eng. tr., 2 vols., London, 1865, i. 41, 397). If this goes, all that is vital and essential in Christianity goes; if this remains, all else remains. And so through the centuries, from Celsus onwards, the Resurrection has been the storm centre of the attack upon the Christian faith.[24]

Brett spoke up. "Earlier, I think it was Jessica who mentioned that Christ predicted His death. I mean, this seems kind of embarrassing for the disciples and Christianity since they didn't get it, doesn't it? Where exactly in the Bible does Jesus predict His death? Can somebody show me those verses?"

Mina was quick to reply. "First of all, from a historical perspective, the embarrassing details of the flaws of the disciples seem to point to the truthfulness of what really happened. If the apostles were making stories up about themselves it seems unlikely they would include so many embarrassing facts about themselves. I mean, for Jesus to tell them over and over that He was going to die and come back from the dead, and they still did not understand it? That's embarrassing! But read from a historical perspective, it adds to the credibility."

Mina took a sip of her vanilla latte and continued, "If a writer is making a story up, he is likely to exaggerate the positive and leave ordinary embarrassments out of it. These Jewish men had been taught in their culture that the Messiah would be a political leader, whereas the cross was seen as the most despicable method of execution anywhere. The idea of their political savior dying on a cross was unthinkable. If you give me a second, I'll look up the references on my computer of Christ predicting His resurrection."

"While you look those up, I'd like to share one more passage I brought showing the significance of the resurrection on the disciples," said Andrea. "This is from Dr. William Lane Craig."

It is difficult to exaggerate what a devastating effect the crucifixion must have had on the disciples. They had no conception of a dying, much less rising, Messiah, for the Messiah would reign forever (cf. John 12:34). Without prior belief in the resurrection, belief in Jesus as Messiah would have been impossible in light of his death.

The resurrection turned catastrophe into victory. Because God raised Jesus from the dead, he could be proclaimed as Messiah after all (Acts 2:32, 36). Similarly for the significance of the cross—it was his resurrection that enabled Jesus' shameful death to be interpreted in salvific terms. Without it, Jesus' death would have meant only humiliation and accursedness by God; but in view of the resurrection it could be seen to be the event by which forgiveness of sins was obtained. Without the resurrection, the Christian Way could never have come into being. Even if the disciples had continued to remember Jesus as their beloved teacher, they could not have believed in him as Messiah, much less deity.[25]

Seven

DID JESUS PREDICT HIS DEATH AND RESURRECTION?

LAUREN LOOKED at Brett. "Brett, some of this Bible stuff is getting annoying. Why does it matter that Christ predicted His resurrection in the New Testament?"

Brett paused before speaking. "From a historical perspective—the bibliographical test is how Jamal put it—the biblical literature seems accurate. Though I'm still skeptical of the resurrection, I think I was proven wrong about the historicity of Christ when Jamal and Dr. Peterson showed me that the New Testament has more manuscripts, earlier manuscripts, and more accurate copies than any other work of antiquity. There are more non-Christian sources that reference Jesus than Caesar. So, from a historical perspective, I would like to investigate and see if perhaps the disciples made it up. Pilate was concerned that the disciples could have stolen the body, and even reading the Bible, I don't remember Jesus telling His disciples time after time that He was going to rise again."

"I think Brett is right, Lauren," said Scott. "From my doctoral work in history, I've known we can't just dismiss this and say, 'Oh, that's in the Bible, we can't take it seriously.' If we take that point of view, we should probably start doubting *everything* in history. I think we should look within the text and see what's there."

"This *is* important," Mina replied, "because Jesus not only predicted His resurrection but also emphasized that His rising from the dead would be the 'sign' to authenticate His claim to be the Messiah. If He were wrong here, He would have been one of the greatest imposters and deceivers of all time. Here are the references I came up with."

Mina turned to her computer and glanced at the references, then passed it to Brett who read out loud:

From that time Jesus began to show His disciples that He must go to Jerusalem, and suffer many things from the elders and chief priests and scribes, and be killed, and be raised up on the third day. (Matthew 16:21 NASB)

"Behold, we are going up to Jerusalem; and the Son of Man will be delivered to the chief priests and scribes, and they will condemn Him to death, and will hand Him over to the Gentiles to mock and scourge and crucify Him, and on the third day He will be raised up." (Matthew 20:18–19 NASB)

As they were coming down from the mountain, He gave them orders not to relate to anyone what they had seen, until the Son of Man rose from the dead. They seized upon that statement, discussing with one another what rising from the dead meant. (Mark 9:9–10 NASB)

The Jews then said to Him, "What sign do You show us as your authority for doing these things?" Jesus answered them, "Destroy this temple, and in three days I will raise it up." The Jews then said, "It took forty-six years to build this temple, and will You raise it up in three days?" But He was speaking of the temple of His body. So when He was raised from the dead, His disciples remembered that He said this; and they believed the Scripture and the word which Jesus had spoken. (John 2:18–22 NASB)

"So Brett, do you believe Jesus died?" asked Andrea.
"Well, yes. I'll admit that He died."
"What about you Scott, Lauren, and Amy?"

They nodded their heads in agreement, but then Lauren commented, "I'm not sure we will ever really know."

Andrea nodded, and then said, "Brett, you believe that Jesus died in history. Do you believe that He rose from the dead?"

"No."

"What happened, then? Why was the tomb empty?"

"I'm not sure. Maybe the peasant women and simple fishermen got the tomb mixed up."

"*Really?*" Andrea shot back. "Do you *really* think that? And what do you mean by *peasant* women? Do you mean they were ignorant? What's your basis for saying that? Sounds chauvinistic to me. Mark, an early source, mentions that the tomb was owned by Joseph of Arimathea, a well-known member of the Sanhedrin and leader in the community. Was he also ignorant? And Peter and John might have been *simple* fishermen, but that doesn't mean they couldn't read or write or speak multiple languages. There's no reason to doubt their intelligence or common sense and assume that all of them were simple folk who got the location of the tomb mixed up. That's a *simple peasant* opinion!"

"Andrea . . ." said Mina.

"It's okay," said Brett. "Maybe I don't really believe that. But I'm sure there's a rational explanation. It seems that what we need to do is investigate the resurrection from a historical perspective. If that evidence points in its favor, then I'll likely become a Christian. However, from the testimony of history and law, I don't think anyone can really know. I'll be willing to research this and meet again next week to share whatever I discover. Are the rest of you willing to study this issue?"

"I guess so," Lauren responded. "Especially if the Christians are open to reading some non-Christian sources. Have you guys read Darwin's *Origin of Species* or Dawkins's *The God Delusion*?"

"I've read them both," Andrea responded immediately. "Duuhhh! I was in your atheist club last year, remember?"

"Mina?"

"I've read most of both books."

"Jessica? Have you read them?"

"I haven't read Dawkins, but I did read part of Darwin in high school."

Lauren couldn't resist taking a jab. "You know tons of Bible verses, but you don't seem that interested in investigating the other side."

"Other side?" Jessica asked. "I was *living* the other side until a year ago. I've only been a Christian for nine or ten months, Lauren. Mina is the only one who has been a Christian for a long time. I suppose I was an atheist since I didn't believe God, but I wasn't really investigating anything thought-provoking. I was just having fun."

Mina spoke up, "I don't mind exploring these books, but they really address a different subject matter. I personally have some questions about Darwinian evolution from a scientific perspective in regard to coding, irreducible complexity, and lack of evidence in the fossil records. But whatever your opinion on Darwin, you still need to wrestle with the historicity of Christ. I mean, there are Christians who disagree on evolution, but evolution doesn't disprove the resurrection. If you think it does, you've moved beyond evolution into a philosophical idea and anti-supernatural bias."

Scott said, "I'm not sure about that anti-supernatural bias part, but I do think you're right in that we should stay on topic and investigate the resurrection from a historical perspective."

"Scott, I really appreciate your open-mindedness," replied Mina. "When an event takes place in history and there are enough people alive who were eyewitnesses of it or who participated in the event, and when the information is published, it should be possible to verify the validity of the event through circumstantial evidences."

"I agree with you, and I'll investigate this with Brett, Amy, and Lauren. Let's meet again in a couple weeks."

Eight

CONSIDERING OTHER POSSIBILITIES

ABOUT A WEEK LATER, Scott headed to the library. He asked Brett to join him, but when Brett showed up, he seemed preoccupied with his advanced chemistry work.

"Sorry I can't help you, Scott, but let me know if you find anything interesting," Brett said from across the table.

Scott left the table for a while and came back with a stack of books. After forty-five minutes of flipping through them, Scott took a deep breath and said, "Interesting."

"What?" Brett asked.

"This is unbelievable. I'm reading a quote from Thomas Arnold, who was the famous headmaster of Rugby, author of the three-volume *History of Rome*, appointed to the chair of modern history at Oxford, and a man well acquainted with the value of evidence in determining historical facts. He said:"

> The evidence for our Lord's life and death and resurrection may be, and often has been, shown to be satisfactory; it is good according to the common rules for distinguishing good evidence from bad. Thousands and tens of thousands of persons have gone through it piece by piece, as carefully as every judge summing up on a most important cause. I have myself done it many times over, not to persuade others but to satisfy myself. I have been used for many years to study the histories of other times, and to examine and weigh the evidence of those who have written about them, and I know of no one fact in the history of mankind which is proved by better and fuller evidence of every sort, to the understanding of a fair inquirer, than the great sign which God hath given us that Christ died and rose again from the dead.[26]

"He was probably biased," Brett remarked.

"Well, maybe so, but I appreciate that he carefully examined it not to persuade others but to satisfy himself. I'm considering committing myself to a similar examination. I've come across several similar conclusions from brilliant philosophers. John Locke, one of the sharpest intellectuals of his century, concluded in his work *A Second Vindication of the Reasonableness of Christianity*,"

> There are some particulars in the history of our Saviour, allowed to be so peculiarly appropriate to the Messiah, such innumerable marks of Him, that to believe them of Jesus of Nazareth was in effect the same as to believe Him to be the Messiah, and so put to express it. The principal of these is His Resurrection from the dead; which being the great and demonstrative proof of His being the Messiah, it is not at all strange that those believing in His Resurrection should be put forth believing Him to be the Messiah, since the declaring His Resurrection was declaring to be the Messiah.[27]

Brett looked at Scott with a smile. "Maybe Jesus didn't die. Muslims believe that there was a substitution and someone else died. Or perhaps they thought He died, but He really survived."

"Come on, Brett. You're playing around, aren't you? You already admitted to Lauren that you believed He died."

"I did. You're right." Brett laughed. "I don't know. I guess there's a chance Jesus lived, but you're right that Jamal and Dr. Peterson told us months ago that even the most skeptical scholars confirm this subject. We should still investigate. Mark was probably the first to write his gospel. What does he say?"

Scott flipped through a Bible to the end of Mark. After skimming a couple pages he read to Brett:

> Wanting to satisfy the crowd, Pilate released Barabbas to them. He had Jesus flogged, and handed him over to be crucified. The soldiers led Jesus away into the palace (that is, the Praetorium) and called together the whole company of soldiers. They put a purple robe on him, then twisted together a crown of thorns and set it on him. And they began to call out to him, "Hail, king of the Jews!" Again and again they struck him on the head with a staff and spit on him. Falling on their knees, they paid homage to him. And when they had mocked him, they took off the purple robe and put his own clothes on him. Then they led him out to crucify him.[28]

"You know, Brett, as a historian, maybe I shouldn't just take Dr. Peterson's or Jamal's word about all scholars holding that Christ died. Maybe there are other explanations. You're right about Muslims believing a switch took place. I'm pretty sure they crucified their intended target, but maybe some of the story has been embellished. Historically, why do people believe this particular method of killing by the Romans took place in Jesus' time? I'm going to check it out right now. Plus, I'm also not so sure about this Joseph of Arimathea that Mina mentioned. He supposedly provided the tomb that Christ was buried in."

"You should check it out, Scott."

They sat for a moment not saying anything. Brett was thinking that he shouldn't leave his friend with all the research, especially since he was the one who dragged Scott into this spiritual conversation with the Christians.

Scott was thinking that he should be doing more research for his upcoming Spanish American history paper. Then again, if he found a more interesting subject, maybe his professor for Ancient Roman History would allow him to switch topics for his graduate paper, even though "crucifixion" was somewhat off the subject matter of that course. But even if his professor wouldn't let him, he had to know the truth. To be intellectually honest, he had to wrestle with the historical Christ. Even if the resurrection was the greatest hoax in history, Scott knew he needed to know what he believed. What *really* happened? Stolen body? Wrong tomb? Disciples made it up? Hallucinations? All these options had to be explored.

Brett broke into his thoughts. "Tell you what, Scott. I'll see if I can learn anything about Christ's crucifixion from a scientific or medical perspective. I doubt it, but we'll see."

In the days that followed, Scott slept little as he passion-
ately pored over research. As he studied, he discovered a
consensus among scholars that Jesus was killed by crucifixion, a common method of Roman execution. Scott took
notes of several disturbing descriptions of this gruesome
practice. Bishop Eusebius of Caesarea, the church historian
of the third century, wrote concerning the Roman scourging
inflicted on those to be executed that the sufferer's "veins
were laid bare, and . . . the very muscles, sinews, and bowels
of the victim were open to exposure."[29] According to the
books Scott researched, many scourging victims failed to
survive the preliminary torture before their crucifixion.

As Scott researched the burial in the tomb of Joseph of
Arimathea, he wanted to get a historical perspective of
tombs and *sepulchers*. Concerning the burial given Christ,
Scott took note of an interesting observation from W. J.
Sparrow-Simpson.

> The Roman practice was to leave the victim of crucifix-
> ion hanging on the cross to become the prey of birds
> and beasts. But who would dream of saying that there
> were no exceptions to this rule? Josephus (*Autobiogra-
> phy*, ch. 75; *Wars of the Jews*, IV, v. 2) induced the
> Emperor Titus to take down from the cross three cruci-
> fied persons while still alive. Would any one argue that
> this cannot be historic because the rule was otherwise?

The Jewish practice, no doubt, was the burial of the condemned. This was the Jewish law. But Josephus assures
us that even the Jews themselves broke the law of burial
at times. In the "Wars of the Jews," he writes: "They pro-
ceeded to that degree of impiety as to cast away their
dead bodies without burial, although the Jews used to
take so much care of the burial of men, that they took
down those that were condemned and crucified, and
buried them before the going down of the sun."

(Some think) that relatives might obtain permission for
burial of one condemned. No relative, however, obtained
it for Jesus' body: nor any of the Twelve. The three crucified men whom Josephus induced the imperial authority to take down from the cross were not relatives; they
were only friends. He "remembered them as his former
acquaintances." A strong case might be made out against
the likelihood of Josephus' request, still more of its being
granted. No one, however, appears to doubt the facts.
They are constantly quoted as if they were true. Why
should not Joseph of Arimathea make a similar request
to Pilate?[30]

Nine

MEDICAL EVIDENCE FOR THE CRUCIFIXION

LATE the following week, Scott and Brett were back in the library. Scott had his Bible open, checking to see if he could discover any contradictions between the biblical accounts and the discoveries of scholars. He was reading about the discovery of Henry Alford, a Greek scholar. Alford noticed, "Matthew alone relates that it was Joseph's own tomb. John, that it was *in a garden*, and *in the place where he was crucified.* All, except Mark, notice the *newness* of the tomb. John does not mention that it *belonged to Joseph.*"[31]

Scott glanced at Brett, who was going through medical journals. *We really should be studying for something that counts.*

Then he caught himself. *But this does count. If the resurrection didn't happen, I want to write a book someday proving to ignorant and deceptive Christians that this is the greatest hoax in history.*

"I don't believe this. Scott!"

"What? Don't believe what?"

"There seems to be quite a lot written on the death of Christ from a medical perspective. An article in the *Journal of the American Medical Association* concluded that according to the gospel accounts, Jesus had died before He was removed from the cross. It states:"

Clearly, the weight of historical and medical evidence indicates that Jesus was dead before the wound to His side was inflicted and supports the traditional view that the spear, thrust between His right ribs, probably perforated not only the right lung but also the pericardium and heart and thereby ensured His death. Accordingly, interpretations based on the assumption that Jesus did not die on the cross appear to be at odds with modern medical knowledge.[32]

Brett continued, "Also, listen to this. Samuel Houghton, M.D., the great physiologist from the University of Dublin, relates his view on the physical cause of Christ's death:

When the soldier pierced with his spear the side of Christ, He was already dead; and the flow of blood and water that followed was either a natural phenomenon explicable by natural causes or it was a miracle. That St. John thought it, if not to be miraculous, at least to be unusual appears plainly from the comment he makes upon it, and from the emphatic manner in which he solemnly declares his accuracy in narrating it. . . . A copious flow of blood, succeeded by a copious flow of water, follows the wound . . . and would occur in a crucified person, who had died upon the cross from rupture of the heart. . . . There remains, therefore, no supposition possible to explain the recorded phenomenon except *the combination of the crucifixion and rupture of the heart.*[33]

"Scott, I was a little hesitant about the apostle John's eyewitness testimony at first, but had to admit that John was giving a correct observation of Christ at Golgotha. He had to be an eyewitness. Listen to this. Dr. Houghton writes:"

The importance of this is obvious. It shows that the narrative in St. John chapter XIX could never have been invented; that the facts recorded must have been seen by an eyewitness; and that the eyewitness was so astonished that he apparently thought the phenomenon miraculous.[34]

Ten

BURIED WITH THE RICH

"SCOTT, from what I'm reading, it seems that only an *eyewitness* of the resurrection would include this unusual medical event. It would make sense that the gospel account of John was really written by Jesus' closest disciple who saw with his own eyes the 'blood and water' flow. Now, it's possible that the carcass of Christ was eaten by vultures, but because the Jews were known to deeply respect the physical body and provide proper burial, I guess that historically it's most likely that Christ was taken down from the cross after dying."

"I can agree with that," said Scott. "From all I am reading, it seems that Mina was right and Christ was buried in the tomb owned by a well-known member of the Sanhedrin named Joseph of Arimathea. In addition, I read a couple scholars who cite a prophecy in Isaiah that the suffering servant would be buried with the rich."

"Yeah, but all those so-called prophecies were written *after the fact*," Brett commented.

"I used to say that too a couple years ago, but we can't use that argument anymore."

"Why not?"

"We have the Septuagint."

"The what?"

"The Septuagint is the Old Testament that was translated from Hebrew into Greek between the second and third century BC. Also, what's strange is that many of the scholars of the Dead Sea Scrolls acknowledge that a copy of the entire scroll of the book of Isaiah was included in the Dead Sea Scrolls, dating around 100 BC. The book of Isaiah itself was written about 700 BC."

"Before Christ."

"Yeah."

"Well, let's look at it, Scott. Most prophecies are so weird and ambiguous that anybody can interpret them to mean whatever they want."

"You're right," Scott said, laughing. "Christians can't even agree with themselves on prophecy. It's all about sheep and bowls and dragons. Probably isn't even real prophecy."

What Scott didn't admit to Brett was that a couple of the prophecies actually seemed to be talking about Christ. For example, he had read a conclusion on Isaiah from Dr. Michael L. Brown, who grew up in a Jewish family and later placed his trust in Jesus. As a student, Dr. Brown investigated Hebrew prophecy, which led him to earn his PhD in Near Eastern Languages and Literatures from New York University. Scott didn't even want to mention this guy to Brett.

Their conversation was suddenly interrupted.

"Hello, Brett," a familiar voice behind him said.

"Dr. Peterson! What a surprise to see you here!" Brett could not believe the university's leading religion professor and former popular skeptic walked right in while they were having this conversation.

"How's the studying going, Brett? And what's this? A premed student becoming a religious scholar? You have an impressive selection of theological works mixed in here with your scientific journals. Are you considering a new course of study?" Dr. Peterson was chuckling.

"Yeah, I mean no, I'm just researching a few things during my free time. We do need to catch up. I've learned much from your insights and I'm still seeking answers to a lot of nagging questions. Oh, by the way, this is my friend Scott. He's pursuing his PhD in history."

"Pleasure to meet you, Scott. And Brett, feel free to stop by the office any afternoon after two if I can be of any help. In fact, this Thursday my wife and I are planning to have a few students over for a barbecue. We would sure enjoy it if you'd both come. I believe you know some of the others, Brett. Jessica Friesen and her friends Mina and Andrea will be there. You're friends with them, right?"

"Oh, yeah, yeah. We still hang out with them. We actually meet to have theological conversations every couple of weeks. I'd love to come over."

"We'll look forward to seeing you, Brett. And Scott, we'd love to have you join us as well."

"Thank you, Dr. Peterson. I'd love to join you all."

"Very good. Come on over and bring friends if you'd like. We'll have plenty of food. I'm grilling chicken and ribs!"

"Dr. Peterson, since you're here, may I ask you a question about something we've been discussing?"

Eleven

A PROPHECY DISCOVERED IN THE DEAD SEA SCROLLS

"YOU CAN certainly ask, and I'll give it my best shot," Dr. Peterson replied.

"Thanks. What do you know about the Dead Sea Scrolls?" asked Brett.

"Well, I've studied them. What specifically would you like to know?"

"I actually don't know very much about them, but Scott just mentioned something about the Septua-gint," Brett answered.

"You mind if I have a seat?" Dr. Peterson seemed to be settling in for a not-so-short response.

"Not at all. Please join us."

Dr. Peterson took off his hat and sat down. He then glanced around to make sure their conversation wouldn't be disturbing any nearby neighbors.

"In the spring of 1947, a young Bedouin shepherd boy was keeping an eye on his sheep one mile west of the north end of the Dead Sea, about seven miles south of Jericho. After tossing a stone at a stray goat he heard the sound of shattering pottery. As first he was frightened, wondering if he had heard an evil spirit. But the next day he came back with his cousins and entered a cave that had been untouched for generations. They discovered jars filled with what looked like leather. The young shepherd thought perhaps he could make some money by selling the leather to be used for shoes, so he took his new discovery to a shoe salesman who happened to be an antiquities dealer on the side. The antiquities dealer, observing the leather, recognized that there were four scrolls inside the protective leather covering, and he bought the scrolls. The dealer turned around and sold the scrolls to an Orthodox archbishop for about two hundred and fifty dollars. After passing through a few more owners, the scrolls were eventually purchased for $250,000, and they are now considered one of the best archeological discoveries of all time."

"Why is that?" Scott asked.

"Ah, good question! First, we learned much about the ancient Jewish sect known as the Essenes. Also, a scroll called 'The Temple Scroll' was discovered that reveals some intriguing details about the construction of the Jerusalem Temple. But to answer your question, there is no doubt that the greatest discovery in this ancient collection was the copy of the entire scroll of Isaiah."

Brett looked at Scott knowing they had just talked about this. However, Scott merely said, "Isaiah?"

Dr. Peterson replied, "Oh yes! One of these Dead Sea Scrolls includes a copy of the entire book of Isaiah, all sixty-six chapters, that dates back to 100 BC. The scroll is twenty-four feet long and is the oldest biblical scroll ever discovered. It is now protected in a vault in Jerusalem, and high-resolution images are available online for public examination. In this ancient copy of Isaiah is a prophecy that has convinced many Jews to place their trust in *Yeshua*."

"*Yeshua?*" Brett asked.

"Yes, that's Hebrew for Jesus. Have you both read Isaiah 53?"

Brett responded first. "No, just some quotes from it."

"Scott?"

"Yeah, I read it once."

"Well, what do you think?"

"Um, I'm not sure." Scott, who knew he was in over his head, wasn't about to debate the issue with Dr. Peterson.

"You're not sure? When you two get the chance, check out Isaiah 53 for yourselves. It should only take a couple minutes, and there are several things to take note of as you're reading. Scholars date the original writing to about 700 BC, at least one hundred years before the implementation of the method of crucifixion on a cross. However, the text speaks of a man of sorrow who would carry many people's transgressions and be pierced for our transgressions and crushed for our iniquities. I personally believe this is one of the most important chapters in the entire Bible, and it provides the best prophetic description of Jesus Christ you will find. It is definitely worth your reading and consideration."

Scott avoided eye contact for a few seconds, knowing that other scholars confirmed what Dr. Peterson was saying.

Dr. Peterson put his hat on and stood up to leave. "Well, I've interrupted your study time long enough. Brett, it sure was good to see you, and Scott, it was a pleasure meeting you. I will look forward to continuing our conversation! Will I see you both on Thursday?"

They nodded.

"Good. Bring some friends."

"Thanks, Dr. Peterson. We'll be there," Brett added, "and I'll invite two friends of ours from the atheist club, Lauren and Amy. Mina and Jessica know them. Lauren mentioned that she wanted to meet with you sometime and ask a few questions. Is that all right?"

"Of course! What better way to spend an evening?"

As Dr. Peterson left, Scott looked at Brett. "How coincidental was that?"

"Well, we *are* near the religious books," Brett responded.

"No, we're *surrounded* by religious books. And he brought up the very chapter we were about to discuss—Isaiah 53!"

"Scott, don't get mystical on me. I brought the subject up by asking what he knew about the Dead Sea Scrolls. And if you've never heard about that prophecy, you've never spent any time around Bible-believing Christians."

"I'm not getting mystical," said Scott. "*You're* the one who is about to become a Christian!"

"Whatever. Are you going to the cookout for real?" Brett asked.

"Yeah, I'll go. It will be fun to ask Dr. Peterson some questions. He's pretty sharp and down-to-earth. Besides, the man really knows how to grill!"

"Okay, before we go, let's take a quick look at that chapter, Isaiah 53."

Scott pulled up Isaiah 53 on an online Bible. "It's not that long. I'll read it to you."

"Go," said Brett.

He grew up before him like a tender shoot,
and like a root out of dry ground.

He had no beauty or majesty to attract us to him,
nothing in his appearance that we should desire him.

He was despised and rejected by men,
a man of sorrows, and familiar with suffering.
Like one from whom men hide their faces
he was despised, and we esteemed him not.

Surely he took up our infirmities
and carried our sorrows,
yet we considered him stricken by God,
smitten by him, and afflicted.

But he was pierced for our transgressions,
he was crushed for our iniquities;
the punishment that brought us peace was upon him,
and by his wounds we are healed.

We all, like sheep, have gone astray,
each of us has turned to his own way;
and the Lord has laid on him
the iniquity of us all.

He was oppressed and afflicted,
yet he did not open his mouth;
he was led like a lamb to the slaughter,

and as a sheep before her shearers is silent,
so he did not open his mouth.

By oppression and judgment he was taken away.
And who can speak of his descendants?
For he was cut off from the land of the living;
for the transgression of my people he was stricken.

He was assigned a grave with the wicked,
and with the rich in his death,
though he had done no violence,
nor was any deceit in his mouth.

Yet it was the Lord's will to crush him and cause him to suffer,
and though the Lord makes his life a guilt offering,
he will see his offspring and prolong his days,
and the will of the Lord will prosper in his hand.

After the suffering of his soul,
he will see the light of life and be satisfied;
by his knowledge my righteous servant will justify many,
and he will bear their iniquities.

Therefore I will give him a portion among the great,
and he will divide the spoils with the strong,

> because he poured out his life unto death,
> and was numbered with the transgressors.
> For he bore the sin of many,
> and made intercession for the transgressors.[35]

Brett looked at Scott. "I can see why they say this is about Jesus. It does sound a bit like Him. Can you show me that portion where it says He was cut off from the living?"

Scott turned the screen so they could both see it.

> For he was cut off from the land of the living;
>   for the transgression of my people he was stricken.

> He was assigned a grave with the wicked,
>   and with the rich in his death,
>   though he had done no violence,
>   nor was any deceit in his mouth.[36]

Brett continued, "It sure sounds like an innocent person was killed for the sake of other people. It even sounds like He was killed alongside criminals and buried in a rich man's tomb. That's pretty specific detail, but here's the deal. Maybe Jesus Christ did come, die on a cross, and get buried in a rich man's tomb. Who cares? That still doesn't prove He rose from the dead. Maybe the disciples felt bad after He died and decided to invent a story to keep the dream alive. I don't know, but I'm still not convinced of the resurrection."

Brett paused, thinking. "Okay, I'll admit Jesus was a real person and probably died on the cross. But I just can't believe He popped out of the tomb a few days later and went around with a smile on His face. Dead men don't come back to flesh-and-blood life again! So . . . He's crucified, they take His body down because that's what Jews did back then, and they place it in a tomb owned by Joseph of Arimathea. Scott, what do you know about the tomb being heavily guarded and then suddenly found empty?"

"Who knows? I'm not sure we can really know, but I'll check into it. What do you think?"

"Not sure. I don't have a problem saying he was buried in a tomb. The burial doesn't prove anything. So if the disciples made up the resurrection part, then we're done. Case closed. No Christianity. Can you stay a little longer? I want to explore this burial and empty tomb deal a little more."

"I'm good for another half hour, then I need to hit the gym. You have time for that?"

"Absolutely."

Twelve

THE BURIAL CUSTOMS OF THE JEWS

AFTER about twenty minutes Scott said, "Hey, listen to this. This is from Dr. Alfred Edersheim, an eminent historian from a Jewish background. He wrote specific details of the burial customs of the Jews:"

Not only the rich, but even those moderately well-to-do, had tombs of their own, which probably were acquired and prepared long before they were needed, and treated and inherited as private and personal property. In such caves, or rock-hewn tombs, the bodies were laid, having been anointed with many spices, with myrtle, aloes, and, at a later period, also with hyssop, rose-oil, and rose-water. The body was dressed and, at a later period, wrapped, if possible, in the worn clothes in which originally a Roll of the Law had been held. The "tombs" were either "rock-hewn," or natural "caves" or else large walled vaults with niches along the sides.[37]

"Interesting, but where are you reading that from?" asked Brett.

"It's a piece cited by William Lane Craig."

"William Lane Craig is a *Christian* philosopher. As in *biased*," Brett stated.

"Why do you say that? You may not agree with his belief in the supernatural, but he has two earned doctorates and has published dozens and dozens of academic articles. He's a highly respected man whose words ought to be seriously considered. He certainly crushed Hitchens when they debated."

"That may be true, but I think Hitchens was drunk that evening," said Brett, grinning.

Scott laughed. "Okay, this is what Craig writes on the careful preservation of graves of Jewish holy men:"

During Jesus' time there was an extraordinary interest in the graves of Jewish martyrs and holy men, and these were scrupulously cared for and honored. This suggests that the grave of Jesus would also have been noted. The disciples had no inkling of any resurrection prior to the general resurrection at the end of the world, and they would therefore not have allowed the burial site of the Teacher to go unnoted. This interest also makes plausible the women's lingering to watch the burial and their subsequent intention to anoint Jesus' body with spices and perfumes (Luke 23:55–56).[38]

"I won't even try to disagree with Craig on that point. He can have it. What else you got?"

"This goes back to Dr. Alfred Edersheim. It's about Christ's burial:"

The proximity of the holy Sabbath, and the consequent need of haste may have suggested or determined the proposal of Joseph to lay the Body of Jesus in his own rock-hewn new tomb, wherein no one had yet been laid. . . . The Cross was lowered and laid on the ground; the cruel nails drawn out, and the ropes unloosed. Joseph, with those who attended him, "wrapped" the Sacred Body, "in a clean linen cloth," and rapidly carried It to the rock-hewn tomb in the garden close by. Such a rock-hewn tomb or cave (*Meartha*) had niches (*Kukhin*), where the dead were laid. It will be remembered, that at the entrance to "the tomb"—and within "the rock"—

there was "a court," nine feet square, where ordinarily the bier was deposited, and its bearers gathered to do the last offices for the Dead.[39]

"So you are confident that the women and disciples knew the exact tomb in which Christ was buried and didn't make it up," Brett observed.

"Yes. I think we can give them that." Scott reached over and grabbed another book in which he had placed a marker. "In discussing the records of Jesus' entombment in Joseph of Arimathea's sepulcher, Dr. Wilbur Smith wrote,"

We know more about the burial of the Lord than we know of any single character in all of ancient history. We know infinitely more about his burial than we do the burial of any Old Testament character, of any king of Babylon, Pharaoh of Egypt, any philosopher of Greece, or triumphant Caesar. We know who took His body from the cross; we know something of the wrapping of the body in spices, and burial clothes; we know the very tomb in which his body was placed, the name of the man who owned it, Joseph, of a town known as Arimathaea. We know even where this tomb was located, in a garden nigh to the place where He was crucified, outside the city walls. We have four records of this burial of our Lord, all of them in amazing agreement, the record of Matthew, a disciple of Christ who was there when Jesus was crucified; the record of Mark, which some say was written within ten years of our Lord's ascension; the record of Luke, a companion of the apostle Paul, and a great historian; and the record of John, who was the last to leave the cross, and, with Peter, the first of the Twelve on Easter to behold the empty tomb.[40]

"Once again, this statement by Smith still doesn't prove the *resurrection*. All these writings prove is that He was crucified and buried. What happened next, we don't know. The disciples could have made up the resurrection story, come back later and stolen the body, or maybe even had a vision or hallucination. Like I've said—dead men just don't come back to life! You know, I'm kind of sick of thinking about all this stuff right now. Let's go play some ball. First game normally starts at five."

"Sounds good," said Scott. "We can talk about this more with Dr. Peterson. I'm going to go check out a couple of these books, and then let's get out of here."

Thirteen

THURSDAY
EVENING
BARBECUE

"DR. PETERSON, these ribs are incredible."

"I'm glad you like them, Scott. You need anything else?"

"I'll need a bath when I'm finished, but right now I'm planning to dig into that grilled chicken."

"Oh, don't be such a pig, Scott!" Jessica said as she and Lauren made their entrance.

"Jessica and Lauren, we're so glad you could make it! Make yourself at home."

"Bill, why don't you have a seat and visit with your students," Susan Peterson said to her husband.

"All right, I will. Why don't you come join us?"

"I will in a minute. You go ahead. I need to wait for these brownies and pies."

Andrea and Jessica smiled as Dr. Peterson kissed his wife on the cheek.

It wasn't long before the conversation turned serious. Many of them had memories of Nick and Jamal at these gatherings. There was one time when Nick started arguing with Jamal about some football thing, and Jamal picked Nick up and above his shoulders and threw him into the pool, fully clothed.

Mina also recalled a story Dr. Peterson told during their summer humanitarian trip to Africa in which Jamal, Amy, and Jessica refused to eat some armadillo stew their host put in front of them.

Dr. Peterson jokingly gave Amy and Jessica a hard time about their rudeness.

After about fifteen minutes, Susan Peterson joined them and the conversation shifted to their friend Nick.

"I remember the very first time Jessica and Nick came over. Nick had so many questions about the reliability of Scripture, and, unfortunately, Bill told him that he could be a good person without believing in all the stories of the Bible. He brought up the variants in the manuscripts and the disputed passages, and it really hurt Nick's faith for a while. Thankfully, Nick didn't just believe every word Bill said. He started checking things out for himself and, thanks in large part to the friendship of Jamal and Mina, Nick eventually returned to the Christian faith with more zeal and passion than anyone I've ever seen."

Dr. Peterson spoke up. "Looking back I am so ashamed at how many students I led away from believing that Christ is the Son of God and that He rose from the dead. It was when Nick flew all the way up to see me at my sister's funeral in Oregon that I began to reconsider the possibility of the resurrection and the existence of heaven. I remember spotting him in the back of the crowded church. It brought tears to my eyes."

"And Bill never cries," remarked Susan.

"I just couldn't believe a student would fly all the way from Texas to Oregon to attend a professor's sister's funeral. It was Nick and Jamal who really challenged me to reinvestigate the historicity of the resurrection."

Susan Peterson looked at Mina. "And Mina, the world needs more people like you. You didn't just live out your faith—you provided good, solid answers for Nick, who was then able to influence my husband. You know, there are so many Christians who claim to love God with their whole hearts, but they are intellectually lazy, shallow in their faith, and too timid to speak up about what they believe. They never provide any good reasons for what or why they believe. I know about this because I was one of them. Mina, the way you love Christ with both your heart and mind has challenged me."

Jessica added, "We love Mina. She challenges all of us."

Andrea nodded in agreement as Jessica continued, "I grew up going to church, and we were told over and over to be passionate for God, but it all seemed so emotional. On Friday night when I didn't feel the presence of God, my faith was gone. I have learned more from Mina in this past year than from all my growing-up years combined."

"You all are so sweet," Mina replied.

Brett glanced at Lauren and Scott, who were sitting together. He could tell they were uncomfortable with all the Christian conversation. He also knew that Dr. Peterson was no stranger to spiritually diverse groups. There was an atmosphere of acceptance in the Peterson home that made people—himself included—feel less defensive than normal, so he decided to toss out a question and spark some lively interaction.

"Dr. Peterson, I don't want to sound like I'm doubting you, but it seems like most Christians only become Christians after something bad happens. Like you when your sister died, or others around campus after the shooting. I know the Scriptures can bring comfort to hurting people, but what if a person wants to believe because it's true, not just because it brings comfort? I am still unconvinced by all this resurrection business, and without that, I don't see where there's anything to believe in."

Fourteen

ELVIS AND MICHAEL JACKSON!

BRETT'S QUESTION FELL like a thud into the conversation, and so he continued talking to explain himself a bit better. "We know the disciples were fickle men who weren't always sure what they believed about Jesus. They sometimes thought He was the Messiah, but they also doubted. Maybe after Jesus died they wanted to keep the dream alive, so they either made up the story or just wanted it to be true and told themselves it was. Lots of people believe in things that aren't real. I mean, look at all the Elvis fans who claim to have seen him walking around in a grocery store. Now there are people who say that Michael Jackson is alive but hiding somewhere. Every celebrity has weird followers with wild imaginations. I think if a man wants to believe something badly enough, he will!"

"Do you know of any Elvis or Michael Jackson fans who are willing to die for what they claim to have seen?" Dr. Peterson calmly asked.

"No, but I'm sure they're probably out there."

"Elvis fans who believe that Elvis was raised from the dead aren't starting a movement with thousands of followers who are willing to die for their belief in his resurrection. Whereas, the apostle Peter stood up on the day of Pentecost in front of a hostile, antagonistic audience and boldly proclaimed the resurrection of Christ. He also reminded them that Jesus had done 'miracles and wonders and signs' in their presence. He literally said to them, 'as you yourselves know.' If his audience didn't think it was true, they would have immediately refuted what he said. But that's not what happened. Three thousand individuals were converted to Christianity that day because they knew what Simon Peter was telling them was true."

Dr. Peterson took a sip of his lemonade and continued, "Brett, I have looked into every possibility, and the resurrection is the best explanation in light of the abundance of evidence. After the resurrection, eleven of the twelve apostles were martyred—not just because of something they believed in, but for something they knew to be true. People may die for a lie they think is true, but they won't die for a lie they know to be false. Last year, when I was still skeptical and reading from the leading scholars on this subject, I remember reading from Dr. Peter Kreeft, a professor of philosophy at Boston College. He asked, 'Why would the apostles lie? . . . If they lied, what was their motive, what did they get out of this? What they got out of it was misunderstanding, rejection, persecution, torture, and martyrdom. Hardly a list of perks.'"[41]

"Dr. Peterson?"

"Yes, Mina."

"Can you please show Scott, Brett, Amy, and Lauren your personal library here at the house? I think Scott, especially, because of his interest in history, would enjoy seeing all of your Latin and Roman texts."

"Good idea. Any of you who would like to see, follow me—and watch your step. My library has a lot of clutter. Susan has been fussing at me for years to get better organized."

Fifteen

THE GUARD
AT THE TOMB

THERE IS NO WAY a personal study could be so large. No wonder Dr. Peterson always has something to talk about! Lauren thought.

Scott was equally impressed. He had never seen a personal library with such a variety of historical texts. He looked at an entire shelf featuring Latin texts, including the works of Cicero and Pliny the Elder's *Naturalis Historia* and *De Architectura*. His curiosity, however, had been brewing all afternoon, so he took his first jab. "Dr. Peterson, you have the largest personal library I have ever seen. I'm more than a little envious. If there is such an abundance of historical evidence for the resurrection of Christ, why did it take you so long to believe? It seems like what Brett said—you came to faith because of emotional reasons rather than intellectual."

Peterson sighed, and was slow to answer. "Not completely, Scott. It was actually on account of emotional reasons that I *didn't* believe for so long. I could never completely escape the dogged feelings of guilt I had from pursuing my own sinful and selfish way of life. Probably my intellectual achievements were the 'god' in my life, and yet inner peace eluded me. Therefore my biblical studies became my escape. I started looking for reasons *not* to believe. I began doubting the minor discrepancies in the papyri text. In early undergraduate studies, I wanted respect from my peers and professors and so I was brash to affirm my commitment to naturalism in my science courses. Years later as a young professor, I felt pressured to get tenure here at Opal and didn't *feel* I could do so if my colleagues believed I was 'narrow-minded,' which generally means believing that Jesus is the only way of salvation. There were also emotional reasons involved in both my season of doubting and then my conversion back to the faith. As Brett pointed out, emotion was clearly a factor when my sister died. However, because such men as Jamal and Nick loved me enough to confront the foundations for my belief system, I had to face the facts I had willfully ignored. My new search for truth wasn't easy. I'm sure you know the saying, 'You can't teach an old dog new tricks.' It took months of reassessing my assumptions and biases against the resurrection to finally trust in Christ. After investigating the historical truth of the resurrection, I am convinced that God truly loves me, just as He loves you."

Scott waited a moment to show respect for the personal nature of Dr. Peterson's comments, and then followed-up with, "Dr. Peterson, you've mentioned the resurrection multiple times. How do you know the disciples didn't take Jesus' body away?"

"Are you familiar with the Roman guard?" Dr. Peterson asked.

"Sort of," Scott replied.

Dr. Peterson walked over to a tall shelf and picked up a large dictionary. "Scott, when it comes to the topic of the Roman guard, William Smith, in the *Dictionary of Greek and Roman Antiquities*, gives us some information about the number of men in a Roman guard. According to Dr. Smith, 'Four was the regular number for a Roman guard . . . of these one always acted as a sentinel, while the others enjoyed a certain degree of repose; ready, however to start up at the first alarm.'"[42]

Dr. Peterson continued, "Matthew, who wrote to the Jews, and by the way, was an eyewitness of the life of Christ, recorded this and mentioned the 'guard.'"

Dr. Peterson picked up a large black Bible from one of his four desks and began reading:

On the next day, which followed the Day of Preparation, the chief priests and Pharisees gathered together to Pilate, saying, "Sir, we remember, while He was still alive, how that deceiver said, 'After three days I will rise.' Therefore command that the tomb be made secure until the third day, lest His disciples come by night and steal Him away, and say to the people, 'He has risen from the dead.' So the last deception will be worse than the first."

Pilate said to them, "You have a guard; go your way, make it as secure as you know how." So they went and made the tomb secure, sealing the stone and setting the guard.[43]

"Scott, there has been discussion concerning whether the 'guard' in this passage speaks of 'temple police' or a Roman guard. A. T. Robertson, the noted Greek scholar, says that the phrase 'Have a guard,' *echete koustodian*, is present imperative and refers to a guard of Roman soldiers, not mere temple police.[44] Robertson further observes that 'the Latin term *koustodia* occurs in an Oxyrhynchus papyrus of AD 22.'"[45]

"Are you *certain* that Pilate was talking about the Roman guard?" Brett asked. "Or are you allowing that it's at least *possible* that Pilate was speaking of the Temple guard?"

"Sure, it's possible, but let me also say that the temple guard was not just one individual officer, but a number of highly disciplined and trained men." Dr. Peterson started flipping through another book from a shelf that also featured a sculpture of Homer.

"Brett, are you familiar with the Jewish historian Alfred Edersheim?"

Brett grinned at Scott and nodded.

"Good. In regards to the identity of the temple guard, Alfred Edersheim documents that a temple guard consisted of ten officers.[46] We know from the Mishnah that there was severe punishment for any temple officer caught sleeping. Let me read from the Oxford University Press translation from 1933."

The officer of the Temple Mount used to go round to every watch with lighted torches before him, and if any watch did not stand up and say to him, "O officer of the Temple Mount, peace be to thee!" and it was manifest that he was asleep, he would beat him with his staff, and he had the right to burn his raiment. And they would say, "What is the noise in the Temple Court?" "The noise of some Levite that is being beaten and having his raiment burnt because he went to sleep during his watch."

R. Eliezar b. Jacob said: "They once found my mother's brother asleep and burnt his raiment."[47]

Dr. Peterson closed the book. "What we know for certain is that this tomb was guarded by a *minimum* of four disciplined men with other disciplined officers aware of their specific task of duty."

Sixteen

THEY ALL FORSOOK HIM AND FLED

LAUREN DECIDED to ask a question. "I'll agree that the body of Jesus was buried in a tomb provided by Joseph of Arimathea, and that it was closely guarded, but I'm still not believing in the resurrection. I mean, couldn't the disciples have made up the resurrection part later?"

"It's doubtful," Dr. Peterson replied.

"*Why* is it doubtful?" Lauren asked, showing some irritation.

"First, when Jesus was in the garden of Gethsemane, Mark writes, 'Then everyone deserted him and fled.'[48] The disciples were not expecting the resurrection. They were fearful of the authorities. Even

Joseph of Arimathea was fearful of the Jews. But what they saw changed them dramatically. Let me read from Dr. J. P. Moreland, who earned his doctorate from the University of Southern California:"

[The disciples] had nothing to gain by lying and starting a new religion. They faced hardship, ridicule, hostility, and martyr's deaths. In light of this, they could have never sustained such unwavering motivation if they knew what they were preaching was a lie. The disciples were not fools and Paul was a cool-headed intellectual of the first rank. There would have been several opportunities over three or four decades of ministry to reconsider and renounce the lie.[49]

"Dr. Peterson," Lauren said, "what happened while the tomb was being guarded?"

"I'll tell you what. Here's a Bible. Read to us from Matthew 28, beginning in verse two."

Lauren took the Bible from Dr. Peterson and read aloud,

And behold, there was a great earthquake; for an angel of the Lord descended from heaven, and came and rolled back the stone from the door, and sat on it. His countenance was like lightning, and his clothing as white as snow. And the guards shook for fear of him, and became like dead men.[50]

Lauren looked up at Dr. Peterson. "Should I keep reading?"

"Yes, Lauren, read verses 11–15," Dr. Peterson replied.

Now while they were going, behold, some of the guard came into the city and reported to the chief priests all the things that had happened. When they had assembled with the elders and consulted together, they gave a large sum of money to the soldiers, saying, "Tell them, 'His disciples came at night and stole Him away while we slept.' And if this comes to the governor's ears, we will appease him and make you secure." So they took the money and did as they were instructed; and this saying is commonly reported among the Jews until this day.[51]

Dr. Peterson took the Bible and set it on his desk. "Lauren, knowing that these guards were highly trained makes the narrative of Matthew 28 very impressive. The sight that coincided with Jesus' resurrection was frightening enough to cause rugged soldiers to 'become like dead men.' Let me read one more description of the Roman guard:"

They had not the slightest interest in the task to which they were assigned. Their sole purpose and obligation was rigidly to perform their duty as soldiers of the empire of Rome to which they had dedicated their allegiance. The Roman seal affixed to the stone before Joseph's tomb was far more sacred to them than all the philosophy of Israel or the sanctity of her ancient creed. They were . . . cold blooded enough to gamble over a dying victim's cloak.[52]

Mina spoke up next. "Dr. Peterson, I remember reading Dr. T. G. Tucker describing in great detail the armor and weapons a centurion would have worn. The picture he gives is of a human fighting machine."[53]

"You're right, Mina."

Lauren wasn't sure what to say, but she wanted to show Dr. Peterson that she was listening. "What you're saying is that, if there was a guard at the tomb after Joseph of the Sanhedrin had Jesus buried, it's unlikely they would have fallen asleep."

"It's very unlikely."

Dr. Peterson picked up another book. "Dr. Thomas Thorburn tells us that the guard that had kept the watch was in dire straits. When the stone was rolled away and the seal broken, they were as good as court-martialed. He writes, 'The soldiers cannot have alleged they were asleep, for they well knew that the penalty of sleeping upon a watch was death—always rigorously enforced.'[54] He continues, 'Here the soldiers would have practically no other alternative than to trust the good offices of the priests. The body (we will suppose) was *gone*, and their negligence in *any* case would (under ordinary circumstances) be punishable by death.'"

Seventeen

THE EMPTY TOMB

"DR. PETERSON, how certain are we that the tomb was empty after this earthquake?" Brett asked. "Let's suppose the disciples experienced hallucinations or dreams of their risen savior. Couldn't the body still have been in the tomb?"

"Have you ever heard of Sir Norman Anderson, who was a lawyer and professor of oriental law at the University of London?" Brett shook his head as Dr. Peterson walked to another shelf and pulled another book.

"Scott? Andrea? Anybody?"

Mina smiled. "I only know because I've heard you reference him before."

Dr. Peterson smiled and adjusted his glasses.

"Sir Norman Anderson was educated at St. Lawrence College and Trinity College, Cambridge, where he took Firsts in undergraduate examinations, and in the Masters. After graduation he traveled to Egypt where he learned Arabic and developed an interest in Islamic and Arabic law. He was instrumental in various posts concerning Arab affairs, and soon became Colonel and Chief secretary of the political section of GHQ Middle East. He was awarded Officer of the Order of the British Empire for these services."

The eight students smiled at each other as Dr. Peterson rambled on, while flipping through his books.

"Returning to England a few years later, Anderson joined the School of Oriental and African Studies, became a Professor in Oriental Law, and eventually served as head of the department for twenty years. Sir Anderson was knighted in 1975, and also traveled to the United States to lecture at universities including Princeton. He was offered professorship for life at Harvard and turned it down. He passed away in the mid-nineties. Do you mind if I read Sir Anderson's conclusion about the empty tomb?"

"Please do," Andrea and Lauren said at the same time.

"Sir Anderson was asked, 'Have you noticed that the references to the empty tomb all come in the Gospels, which were written to give the Christian community the facts they wanted to know?' Dr. Anderson responded, 'In the public preaching to those who were not believers, as recorded in the Acts of the Apostles, there is an enormous emphasis on the fact of the resurrection but not a single reference to the empty tomb. Now, why? To me there is only one answer: There was no point in arguing about the empty tomb. Everyone, friend and opponent, knew that it was empty. The only questions worth arguing about were why it was empty and what its emptiness proved.'"[55]

Dr. Peterson continued, "Sir Anderson also said this about the empty tomb:

The empty tomb stands, a veritable rock, as an essential element in the evidence for the resurrection. To suggest that it was not in fact empty at all, as some have done, seems to me ridiculous. It is a matter of history that the apostles from the very beginning made many converts in Jerusalem, hostile as it was, by proclaiming the glad news that Christ had risen from the grave—and they did it within a short walk from the sepulcher. Any one of their hearers could have visited the tomb and come back again between lunch and whatever may have been the equivalent of afternoon tea. Is it conceivable, then, that the apostles would have had this success if the body of the one they proclaimed as risen Lord was all the time decomposing in Joseph's tomb? Would a great company of the priests and many hard-headed Pharisees have been impressed with the proclamation of a resurrection which was in fact no resurrection at all, but a mere message of spiritual survival couched in the misleading terms of a literal rising from the grave?[56]

"The majority of all scholars agree with Anderson. Recently, I read an observation from Dr. J. P. Moreland, which I have here somewhere . . ."

Scott was walking around the room reading titles and shaking his head.

"Okay, here we are. J. P. Moreland writes, 'In sum, the absence of explicit mention of the empty tomb in the speeches in Acts is best explained by noting that the fact of the empty tomb was not in dispute and thus it was not at issue. The main debate was over why it was empty, not whether it was empty. . . . No need existed for the early Christian preachers to make a major issue of the empty tomb. It was common knowledge which could be easily verified if such verification was needed.'"[57]

Eighteen

THE IMPORTANCE OF APPEARANCES

BRETT DECIDED to take another tack. "Let's say there's some reasonable explanation as to why the tomb is empty. Can you give us any other evidences of the resurrection?"

Dr. Peterson walked to where Scott was standing and selected another book. "Let me read from Dr. John Warwick Montgomery, who made this observation:"

Note that when the disciples of Jesus proclaimed the resurrection, they did so as eyewitnesses and they did so while people were still alive who had had contact with the events. In 56 AD

Paul wrote that over 500 people had seen the risen Jesus and that most of them were still alive. That's a reference to 1 Corinthians 15:6. It passes the bounds of credibility that the early Christians could have manufactured such a tale and then preached it among those who might easily have refuted it simply by producing the body of Jesus.[58]

Scott spoke up next. "Who are all these people you're quoting? I've never heard of John Warwick Montgomery."

Dr. Peterson looked at the back inside flap of the book cover. "Scott, Montgomery holds ten earned degrees, including his AB with Distinction from Cornell, Master of Philosophy in Law from the University of Essex, an LLM from Cardiff University, Wales, a PhD from the University of Chicago, a Doctorate from University of Strasbourg, France, and an LLD in canon law from Cardiff University. Quite an academic background!"

"It seems to me," Brett said, "that the resurrection appearance stories just don't add up with each other. Some of the testimonies speak of the women. Some don't. What were the real appearances?"

Dr. Peterson didn't miss a beat. He walked to his primary desk, picked up a three-ring binder, and opened to one of the tabs. "These are some of my notes from working through this process myself over the past year. This is a list

I compiled showing Jesus' multiple post-resurrection appearances." He handed the notebook to Brett, who read:

- To Mary Magdalene: Mark 16:9; John 20:14
- To women returning from the tomb: Matthew 28:9–10
- To Peter later in the day: Luke 24:34; 1 Corinthians 15:5
- To the Emmaus disciples: Luke 24:13–33
- To the apostles without Thomas: Luke 24:36–43; John 20:19–20
- To the apostles with Thomas present: John 20:26–29
- To the seven by the lake of Tiberias: John 21:1–23
- To the multitude of over 500 believers on a Galilean mountain: 1 Corinthians 15:6
- To James: 1 Corinthians 15:7
- To the eleven: Matthew 28:16–20; Luke 24:33–52
- To a group of disciples at the ascension: Acts 1:3–12
- To Paul: Acts 9:3–6; 1 Corinthians 15:8
- To Stephen: Acts 7:55
- To Paul in the temple: Acts 22:17–21; 23:11
- To John on Patmos: Revelation 1:10–19

Dr. Peterson continued, "Brett, even in journalism, the omission of an individual or detail is not necessarily the denial. Some of the alleged contradictions are easier to explain than I originally thought. For example, Paul and the evangelists might not have mentioned the appearances to women because women's testimony was not considered valid in the court of law during that day. Also, the fact that the gospel accounts testify to the appearances of Christ to the women indicates that they really happened. The story is simple and lacks the legendary embellishment of the second-century Gnostic gospels."

Susan Peterson came in. "Sorry to interrupt, but I have some desserts and coffee outside for anyone who would like some."

"Sounds great!" replied Scott.

Brett spoke up, "I testify to the fact that desserts have a strong appeal to me!"

Nineteen

SPIRITUAL BODIES

AS THE STUDENTS SAT on the back porch around the brazier, conversation continued along the themes of Jesus' resurrection, heaven, and the afterlife. Mina and Jessica shared stories about Nick and Jamal, and Andrea asked Dr. Peterson some questions about heaven, honestly expressing her doubts and struggles. She talked about death—not only of Nick and Jamal, but of a close cousin who had died recently in a car accident. Scott and Lauren were curious about the nature of the resurrected body and wondered if a resurrection were to occur, if perhaps it would be some kind of *spiritual* resurrection. Lauren had once heard a speaker on Oprah's show talking about everyone being transformed after death into spiritual light beings—something like angels.

Andrea asked, "Doesn't Paul call our resurrected bodies 'spiritual bodies'?"

Dr. Peterson responded, "The New Testament authors fully agree that Jesus appeared in bodily, physical form. It should be noted that when Jesus was seen in His spiritual body, it was not entirely the same as His earthly body. But Jesus still had a spiritual *body*, and neither Paul nor the gospel writers understand this to mean a purely spiritual being who is like some 'light being' or a vaporous ghost who still hangs around the earth. The body of Jesus could be physically seen and touched, and was never distinguished as something other than the body laid in the tomb."

"So Dr. Peterson, right now, are Jamal and Nick in 'bodily form' with Christ?" Jessica asked.

"They are certainly with God in spirit, and have a bodily state. However, Scripture tells us that their same body that died will be raised again to life and transformed."

"I hope I get a completely different body in heaven!" Andrea commented with a smile.

"And I certainly hope mine has more hair!" Dr. Peterson quickly replied. "Actually, I have a book that talks about this."

Susan Peterson rolled her eyes. "He *always* has another

book. I wish he put them all on his iPad that I bought him for his birthday. His office has too many books!"

Dr. Peterson returned with the book and began reading,

But while it is true that Paul teaches that our resurrection bodies will be modeled after Jesus' body and they will be spiritual, it does not follow that these bodies will be nonphysical. Such an interpretation is not supported by an exegesis of Paul's teaching. If by *soma pneumatikon* ("spiritual body") one understands a body that is intangible, unextended, or immaterial, then it is false to assert that Paul taught that we shall have that *kind* of resurrection body. New Testament commentators agree that a *pneumatikos* means "spiritual" in the sense of orientation, not substance (cf. 1 Cor. 2:15; 10:4). The transformation of the earthly body to a soma *pneumatikon* accordingly does not rescue it from materiality, but from mortality.[59]

Dr. Peterson leaned in closer to the brazier and flipped the page.

A *soma* ("body") that is unextended and intangible would have been a contradiction in terms for the apostle. The resurrection body will be an immortal, powerful, glorious, Spirit-directed body, suitable for inhabiting a renewed creation. All commentators agree that Paul did not teach the immortality of the soul alone; but his affirmation of the resurrection of the body becomes vacuous and indistinguishable from such a doctrine unless it means the tangible, physical resurrection. The exegetical evidence does not, therefore, support a bifurcation between Paul and the Evangelists with regard to the nature of the resurrection body.[60]

"I'm not sure how you can believe all this," said Lauren. "I'm glad the idea of life after death gives you meaning and comfort, but I think it's a lot of wishful thinking and takes a great leap of faith to believe."

Twenty

PAUL
AND HIS
ENEMIES

MINA REPLIED, "Okay, Lauren. Let's be honest about what you're saying. You still haven't provided a refutation of excellent historical and logical evidence. Nobody has! In fact, the enemies of Christ gave no refutation of the resurrection. They were either silent or they mocked, but they didn't provide a good explanation."

"What do you mean?" Brett asked.

"Well, some of the early enemies were silent and they were in a better position to disprove these claims about Jesus than anyone in history. In Acts 2, Peter stood up on the day of Pentecost and boldly proclaimed the resurrection in front of an antagonistic crowd. There was not one bit of refutation given by the Jews. Why not? Because the evidence of the empty tomb was there for all to examine if they wanted to disclaim it, and yet no one did. Peter also tells this crowd that they were aware of the miracles of Christ, and rather than refuting him, many of them actually became Christians that day!"

Mina pulled up the Bible on her phone and continued. "Brett, in Acts 25, Paul was imprisoned in Caesarea. Festus, who was in charge of the proceedings, 'convened the court and ordered that Paul be brought before him. When Paul appeared, the Jews who had come down from Jerusalem stood around him, bringing many serious charges against him, which they could not prove.'[61] What was it about Paul's gospel that so irritated the Jews? What point did they totally avoid in making their accusations? Festus, in explaining the case to King Agrippa, describes the central issue as concerning 'a certain Jesus, who had died, whom Paul affirmed to be alive.'[62] The Jews could not explain the empty tomb and it just irked them. They made all kinds of personal attacks on Paul, but avoided the *objective evidence* for the resurrection."

Mina continued, "The other most popular response is that the opponents 'mocked.' When Paul went to Athens to talk to the Epicurean and Stoic philosophers about Christ, they had no answer for his claims. Luke documents that 'when they heard of the resurrection of the dead, some mocked.'[63] Like the new atheists, they laughed it off because they could not understand how a man could rise from the dead. They didn't even attempt to rationally defend their position."

Lauren rolled her eyes. "Whatever, Mina."

"Oh, I forgot to tell you the rest about Festus and Agrippa," Mina said.

"Do we have any proof that Festus and Agrippa were real people in history?" Lauren jabbed.

"Actually, we do," Scott replied. "Their existence is a historical fact. I've checked into it."

"Well, never mind then." Lauren wasn't sure she wanted to hear more.

But Mina continued, "Paul told Agrippa and everyone in the court that Christ 'would suffer and, as the first to rise from the dead, would proclaim light to his own people and to the Gentiles.'[64] While Paul was saying this in his defense, Festus shouted at him. Here's how that went:"

At this point Festus interrupted Paul's defense. "You are out of your mind, Paul!" he shouted. "Your great learning is driving you insane."

"I am not insane, most excellent Festus," Paul replied. "What I am saying is true and reasonable. The king is familiar with these things, and I can speak freely to him.

I am convinced that none of this has escaped his notice, because it was not done in a corner. King Agrippa, do you believe the prophets? I know you do."

Then Agrippa said to Paul, "Do you think that in such a short time you can persuade me to be a Christian?"[65]

As Brett listened to Mina talk about the silence and mockery of the critics, he thought that there just had to be another explanation. He reflected about the Discovery Channel special, produced by James Cameron, that he had seen a few years previously. Brett was determined to find another explanation.

As the evening closed and the students talked about other topics, Dr. Peterson invited any who wanted to join them for church and lunch during Easter Sunday in two weeks.

Lauren thought that since she wouldn't be flying back to California, perhaps it would be nice to go to church. She had just bought several new dresses and there was always something about Easter Sunday that made her feel sentimental and hopeful.

Scott was wondering how to respond to the invitation. "Tell you what. I just think we need to make sure that we're looking at 'both sides of the coin.'" It was obvious he was a little frustrated and felt like he and Lauren and Brett were getting ganged up on. "I'll visit your church on Easter

Sunday if some of you would be willing to watch a video showing another side. I also would like to invite Dr. Clayton Ingraham who spoke at our atheist club. I was already planning to meet Dr. Ingraham next Wednesday to ask him some theological questions. Tell you what. My condo is right near campus. Why don't you all come over on Wednesday and we can watch about twenty minutes of James Cameron's *The Lost Tomb of Jesus*, and then maybe we can talk about some other objections to the resurrection."

Andrea reacted instantly. "Scott, do you really mean it?! James Cameron? Are you kidding me? Do you believe in blue Avatars too!?"

Mina quickly replied, "Andrea, be nice. This could make for some fun conversation about the Talpiot tomb and the ossuaries. Let's watch a few minutes and then have some dialogue about the objections Dr. Ingraham is likely to bring up. I will respectfully say, Scott, that few scholars outside of maybe James Tabor believe in the legitimacy of this supposed tomb of Jesus, but I'm sure Ingraham is aware of the objections and perhaps we'll have some lively discussion. Dr. Peterson, can you make it?"

"I'm sorry. Not that evening, but thank you for the invitation. Susan and I have a dinner to attend, but please send Clayton my greetings. We've been friends for years."

Twenty-One

JAMES CAMERON AND THE LOST TOMB OF JESUS

ON WEDNESDAY evening about a dozen students, along with Dr. Clayton Ingraham, gathered at Scott's condominium. Though not large, his open room with the fifty-inch flat screen provided a nice atmosphere for the students to watch part of James Cameron's film and have dialogue afterwards.

As the film began, Mina started typing notes on her laptop. She had already watched it earlier in the week and taken notes, but she kept noting new issues. She also searched "The Lost Tomb of Jesus" on the Discovery Channel's website. As the rest of the students watched the film, Mina skimmed the site. It read:

Since the I970s, hundreds of tombs and thousands of ossuaries (limestone bone boxes) have been discovered in the Jerusalem area. These ossuaries served as coffins in first-century Jerusalem. One of these tombs was found to contain ten ossuaries. Six of the ossuaries in this tomb have inscriptions on them. As it turns out, every inscription in this particular tomb relates to the Gospels. In the feature documentary, *The Lost Tomb of Jesus*, a case is made that the 2,000-year-old "Tomb of the Ten Ossuaries" belonged to the family of Jesus of Nazareth. All leading epigraphers agree about the inscriptions. All archaeologists confirm the nature of the find. It comes down to a matter of statistics. A statistical study commissioned by the broadcasters (Discovery Channel/Vision Canada/C4 UK) concludes that the probability factor is in the order of 600 to I that an equally "surprising" cluster of names would arise purely by chance under given assumptions. The film also documents DNA extraction from human residue found in two of the ossuaries and reveals new evidence that throws light on Jesus' relationship with Mary Magdalene.[66]

Scott fast-forwarded to some of the most important parts of the film, contending that the very bones of Jesus Christ had been discovered.

When the film was over, Brett commented, "It looks like a viable alternative. Once again, I have to say I find it hard to believe that this man, Jesus Christ, was really raised from the dead. Dr. Ingraham, what do you think?"

"Well, this is not my favorite alternative to the resurrection," Dr. Ingraham slowly replied.

"What is your favorite?" Amy asked.

"There are several better explanations we can get into later."

"Dr. Ingraham, what do you think about the Discovery Channel statistical study that concluded the probability factor was six hundred to one against an equally 'surprising' cluster of names arising purely by chance?" asked Andrea.

She must have been taking notes too, thought Mina.

"I'm not a Christian, but I think the 1 in 600 statistic is flawed. I even remember reading an article on Skepticon that questioned this statistic for a number of reasons. I know my colleague James Tabor will disagree with me, but there are many other non-theists like William Dever, who earned his doctorate at Harvard, who question the reliability of this film, simply from a historical basis."

Mina spoke up. "Scott, I'm on Dr. Gary Habermas's

website and have some conclusions from Dr. Habermas and Dr. Ben Witherington. May I read some of them?"

"Go ahead," Scott replied.

Mina began, "Dr. Ben Witherington, New Testament professor at Asbury Theological Seminary and author of *What Have They Done With Jesus?*, had this to say:

> [The Lost Tomb of Jesus] will make good TV but involves a bad critical reading of history. Basically, this is old news with a new interpretation. We have known about this tomb since it was discovered in 1980. There are all sorts of reasons to see that this is much ado about nothing much.[67]

"Then, from Dr. Habermas:

> An incredible number of problems are present in the recent claim that Jesus' grave has been found. In the end, the time-honored, multi-faceted evidence for the Gospel data of the Deity, death, and bodily resurrection of Jesus are more convincing than ever. Even the early opponents of the Christian message acknowledged that Jesus' tomb was empty. And the evidence for Jesus' bodily resurrection appearances has never been refuted.[68]

"There's actually a list of objections here," Mina observed. "Let me read a few of them:"

- The names "Joseph" and "Jesus" were very popular in the first century. "Jesus" appears in at least 99 tombs and on 22 ossuaries. "Joseph" appears on 45 ossuaries.
- "Mary" is the most common female name in the ancient Jewish world.
- The DNA evidence establishes no positive links in this tomb whatsoever.
- The statistical comparison to Jesus of Nazareth is severely flawed.
- There is no early historical nor tomb connection to Mary Magdalene.
- There is no historical evidence anywhere that Jesus ever married or had children.
- The "Jesus" in the tomb was known as "Son of Joseph," but the earliest followers of the New Testament Jesus didn't call him that.
- It is unlikely that Jesus' family tomb would be located in Jerusalem.
- The Talpiot tomb was costly. It apparently belonged to a wealthy family.
- The tenth ossuary has been accounted for without recourse to the "James" ossuary.
- All ancient sources agree that, very soon afterwards, the burial tomb of Jesus of Nazareth was empty.
- The Talpiot tomb data fail to account for Jesus' resurrection appearances.[69]

As Mina rattled off more information, Scott and Lauren looked to Dr. Clayton Ingraham to bring some rebuttal. Since Dr. Ingraham didn't say anything, Lauren thought it was best to change the subject.

Twenty-Two

CHRISTIANITY AND PAGAN MYTHOLOGY

"LOOK, MAYBE Cameron's film isn't exactly right, but there are certainly naturalistic explanations to this so-called resurrection. Perhaps it's just a myth patterned after the various 'dying and rising' fertility gods of ancient pagan religions like Osiris, Adonis, Isis. This resurrection thing could all just be derived from mystery pagan religions."

"I'd like to address this one," Andrea responded. "A year ago, when I was a professing atheist, some of you will recall that I was once convinced of this theory popularized by Internet skeptics. After talking with Jamal and investigating, I discovered that many of the supposed 'parallels' between the Christian doctrine of the resurrection and the dying and rising pagan gods are greatly exaggerated. As a matter of fact, many times critics describe pagan rituals in language they borrowed from Christianity! Words like 'baptism' and 'resurrection' are often uncritically assigned to the acts of pagan deities, even when they have little in common with Christian beliefs. The chronology doesn't support an early Christian dependence on the mystery religions. Mina, do you have anything to add?"

"Only that it's highly, highly unlikely that Paul—with his strict monotheism and Jewish roots—would have borrowed from pagan religions. Also, the death and resurrection of Jesus Christ took place within history, at a historically specified time and place."

Brett asked, "Are you all familiar with the 'wrong-tomb' theory taught by Professor Kirsopp Lake, who teaches that the women did not know where Jesus was buried and mistakenly went to the wrong tomb? As a result of arriving at an empty tomb, they were convinced that Jesus had resurrected."[70]

Mina was quick to reply, "First, his theory ignores all the evidence. Second, it constructs the theory entirely according to a preconceived notion. I was anticipating some of the popular objections such as this one, the legend theory, and the hallucination theory, so I wrote down some answers from leading scholars."

Mina opened up a Word document on her computer. "Dr. William Lane Craig points out that 'if the resurrection was a colossal mistake based on the women's error, then the enemies of Christianity would have been more than happy to point that out, indicating where the correct tomb was or maybe even exhuming a body. The idea that the resurrection stemmed from the women's going to the wrong tomb is too shallow.'[71] Brett, you and Scott know from your studies that alternative theories must account for all of the facts. So let's take the wrong-tomb theory to its logical conclusion. If the women went to the wrong tomb, then you would have to say the men also went to the wrong tomb, and so did the Jews, the Romans, and, I guess you'd have to say the angels went to the wrong tomb. Brett, for me, that is really far-fetched. The wrong-tomb theory does not account for the conversions of Paul or James."

Charles, one of Brett's friends from the atheist club, commented, "This resurrection stuff has to be a legend. You know how it is—you tell a story enough times and wait long enough and you end up with a greatly exaggerated version of the original."

Andrea replied, "But wouldn't this be impossible? Resurrection accounts were circulated and written down by the original eyewitnesses. Paul related in the mid-50s AD there were more than five hundred firsthand eyewitnesses still alive. And this was already well-known within three to eight years of the time of Christ."

"Three to eight years of the time of Christ? What's that about?" said Brett.

Mina quickly replied, "Yes, the passage that included 'creedal language' in 1 Corinthians was probably in circulation within just a few years of the resurrection of Christ. Scholars have identified what they believe are at least portions of early Christian creedal confessions that were formulated and passed on verbally years before they were recorded in the books of the New Testament. As apologist Gary Habermas explains, these affirmations 'preserve some of the earliest reports concerning Jesus from about AD 30–50. Therefore, in a real sense, the creeds preserve pre-New Testament material, and are our earliest sources for the life of Jesus.'[72] In other words, these saying were memorized and passed down orally."

Mina began reading lecture notes that Jamal had emailed her last year. "Over ninety percent of all published scholars on the resurrection in the last thirty years, including the most liberal scholars at Ivy League institutions, admit the early dating of 1 Corinthians, between AD 53 and 57, and second, scholars admit that *Paul* is the real author."

Mina continued, "One of the creedal confessions is in 1 Corinthians 15:3–5. It reads like this, 'For what I received I passed on to you as of first importance: that Christ died for our sins according to the Scriptures, that he was buried, that he was raised on the third day according to the Scriptures, and that he appeared to Peter, and then to the Twelve.'"

Lauren looked at Dr. Ingraham, who had been surprisingly silent so far. "Professor Ingraham, what's your favorite alternative explanation?"

Twenty-Three

THE HALLUCINATION THEORY

"WELL, MANY OF THEM have merit, but I personally appreciate the hallucination theory. I also tend to think the body was stolen. I'm not fully convinced, but I agree that the eyewitnesses of Paul, Peter, and the disciples thought they saw a resurrected Christ. The key word here is 'thought.'"

Lauren and Amy smiled at each other. Maybe their champion for atheism was getting ready to explain all. Mina, Andrea, and Jessica also smiled at each other, because they had read several of Ingraham's articles and knew he had researched this objection extensively.

"Let's also keep in mind that the disciples weren't the sharpest bunch," Dr. Ingraham continued with a grin. "The word 'hallucination' is an anglicized form of the Latin *alucination*, which means 'a wandering of the mind, idle talk, prating.'[73] Medical and psychological observations agree that a hallucination is an apparent act of vision for which there is no corresponding external object. Hallucinations result from purely inner psychological causes—not from the presence of an actual external object. They are subjective visions. It's likely that these disciples *thought* they saw something that really wasn't there."

Andrea spoke up first. "In general, Dr. Ingraham, isn't it only particular kinds of people who have hallucinations—usually paranoid or schizophrenic individuals, patients nearing death, or those under the influence of drugs?"

"Well, that often seems to be the case. The uneducated bunch of eccentrics that Jesus surrounded Himself with seemed a little paranoid to me," Dr. Ingraham replied.

Mina interjected, "It actually seems that we have all different kinds of people from different backgrounds, ages, and occupations claiming to have seen the risen Jesus."

Andrea continued, "Dr. Ingraham, hallucinations are linked to an individual's subconscious and past experiences, making it very unlikely that two or more persons could have the same hallucination at the same time. Christ appeared to multiple people, and descriptions of these varied appearances involve great detail, which psychologists would regard as good indicators that those individuals were in contact with reality."

Dr. Ingraham just smiled as the young ladies talked.

Andrea glanced around the room to see reactions, but continued talking, "I'd like to read a conclusion from clinical psychologist Dr. Gary Collins. 'Hallucinations are individual occurrences. By their very nature only one person can see a given hallucination at a time. They certainly are not something which can be seen by a group of people. . . . Since a hallucination exists only in the subjective, personal sense, it is obvious that others cannot witness it.'[74]

"Collins concluded that the evidence against the hallucination hypothesis is so convincing that skeptics 'would have to go against so much of the current psychiatric and psychological data about the nature of hallucinations.'"[75]

Mina continued, "Dr. Ingraham, I've read your articles and studied the nature of hallucinations. They are usually restricted as to when and where they can happen. In the New Testament situations, favorable circumstances are missing. And the appearances recorded are much more than simple glimpses. Time was involved. We have a record of fifteen different appearances, and one of those was to more than five hundred people."

Dr. Ingraham's silence suddenly turned to irritation. "Are you Christians implying that one has to believe in the literal resurrection of Jesus or be damned to hell? What about all the other religions?" Now he was raising his voice. "What about all the children who grow up learning that Islam is true. Are they going to hell, Mina? There are almost a billion Muslims who sincerely believe that Christ didn't even die on the cross. I think Christians who believe that Jesus Christ is the only way are some of the most intolerant, bigoted people in the whole world."

"Great points!" Lauren applauded.

Mina spoke carefully. "You have brought up several objections to Christianity, but you're changing the subject. The issue of salvation and who goes to heaven is another big topic in itself, and worthy of discussion. But right now we are trying to explain, from a historical standpoint, what is the most reasonable explanation for the empty tomb of Christ and His post-resurrection appearances. You said that the views of Islam on the crucifixion and resurrection of Christ are quite opposite of the traditional Christian view. One view has to be right and one view wrong. It is impossible that Jesus of Nazareth both died and didn't die on the cross."

"Dr. Ingraham," asked Lauren, "what exactly do the Muslims believe about the death of Christ?"

"Friends, the Qur'an claims that Jesus was not crucified on the cross," Dr. Ingraham stated. "Rather than allowing Jesus, one of Allah's servants, to be crucified, Allah is said to have respected his prophet and saved Him by crucifying a bystander who was made to appear to be Jesus. This is known as the 'substitution theory.' Typically, Judas Iscariot or Simon of Cyrene is understood to be the substitute for Jesus. Instead of being crucified, Jesus ascended to heaven, where He remains alive until His return to earth before the end of time."

"Do you believe this theory, Dr. Ingraham?" Jessica asked.

"Not necessarily, but I just want Christians to know that there are other schools of thought."

"Dr. Ingraham," said Mina, "I reject the Muslim substitution theory based on historical problems. There are virtually no scholars today not already committed to Islamic theology who accept this theory. Historically, we have no evidence of this theory for the first several hundred years following the resurrection. The Old Testament predicted the Messiah's death, and so by dying, Jesus fulfilled those prophecies. We have a preserved copy of the scroll of Isaiah that includes the prophecies Jesus fulfilled, discovered with the Dead Sea Scrolls, that predates the event by over one hundred years.

"In addition, Jesus predicted His own death. I remember reading from Dr. Michael Licona that there is agreement among scholars—including skeptical scholars—that Jesus told the parable in Mark 12 which describes a beloved son who is murdered at the hands of evil farmers. It is clear Jesus is talking about His own rejection and future death at the hands of the Jewish people.[76] Since Jesus predicted His own violent death and Muhammad regarded Him as a prophet, if Jesus did not die a violent death He would be a false prophet, a fact that would be anathema to both Christians and Muslims. And, if this is so, then the Qur'an must be wrong, since it claims He escaped death by crucifixion."[77]

Lauren was clearly frustrated. "Mina, you Christians are so intolerant and judgmental of other beliefs. You shouldn't be going around all the time calling everyone else wrong."

"So are you saying that my conclusions are right?" asked Mina.

"No!" Lauren raised her voice.

Mina smiled.

Twenty-Four

THE CONSPIRACY THEORY

DR. INGRAHAM spoke up. "Although, I may not fully agree with James Cameron's film, there are a number of scholars who believe that the followers of Jesus stole His body and fabricated the resurrection story. This theory was even noted in Matthew's gospel.[78] The guards at the tomb went to the Jewish high priest to report what happened. The high priest bribed the Roman guards and told them to spread the lie that the disciples had stolen the body of Jesus. In return, the high priest protected the guards by smoothing things over with Pilate." As Dr. Ingraham spoke, he was pulling up some historical references on his laptop.

"Mina, according to Justin Martyr, in his Dialogue Against Trypho #108, around AD 130, the story was being told: 'One Jesus, a Galilean deceiver, whom we crucified, but his disciples stole him by night from the tomb, where he was lain when unfastened from the cross, and now deceive men by asserting that he has risen from the dead and ascended to heaven.'"[79]

Jared, another atheist, interjected with excitement, "That confirms what I've thought all along—the disciples conspired together and stole the body!"

Mina, accustomed to this popular objection, had already bookmarked several responses. Referring to research on her computer, she commented, "Dr. Ingraham, you ought to know that this conspiracy theory was refuted by the great historian Eusebius in his *Deomonstratio Evangelica.* Eusebius argues that it is inconceivable that such a well-planned and thought-out conspiracy could ever succeed. Eusebius gives a satirical speech that he imagines to have been delivered by the disciples in efforts to motivate each other:"

Let us band together to invent all the miracles and resurrection appearances which we never saw and let us carry the shame even to death! Why not die for nothing? Why dislike torture and whipping inflicted for no good reason? Let us go out to all nations and overthrow their institutions and denounce their gods! And even if we don't convince anybody, at least we'll have the satisfaction of drawing down on ourselves the punishment for our own deceit.

"It's seems that Eusebius is implying that if we distrust the disciples, then we must distrust all writers of history!" Andrea stated.

Dr. Ingraham folded his arms as Mina continued talking. "The news media continually shows us that conspiracies normally unravel. Either the opponents uncover the truth or someone on the inside slips or gives in to pressure. Dr. Ingraham, can I please read another conclusion from Chuck Colson, Special Counsel to President Nixon during the Watergate scandal?"

"I really don't see how it applies, but go ahead and read it!"

"Thanks. Colson wrote, 'I know how impossible it is for a group of people, even some of the most powerful people in the world, to maintain a lie. The Watergate cover-up lasted only a few weeks before the first conspirator broke and turned state's evidence.'[80] As soon as pressure mounted and the Watergate conspirators realized they could be punished, they broke. Yet in contrast, not even one of Jesus' disciples, even though they faced horrendous persecution and death, renounced his belief in the resurrection of Jesus."

Jessica addressed Jared, "Jared, you also mentioned that

the disciples stole the body. How was that possible?"

"Well after a long night of killing Jesus, the soldiers were probably worn out and fell asleep," Jared replied.

"I learned from Dr. Peterson that the discipline and accountability of Roman soldiers was similar to that of Navy SEALS. In light of the remarkable discipline of the Roman army, isn't it ludicrous to believe that a team of highly trained guards fell asleep on duty while a group of timid fishermen quietly broke the seal, rolled the boulder aside, picked up Jesus' body, and carried it away? Remember, these are men who ran from the Garden at the first sign of trouble, and the bravest among them cursed and swore to a servant girl that he didn't even know Jesus."

"Dr. Peterson told you this, did he?" Dr. Ingraham sighed. "My, how he's changed his beliefs. He even invited me to go to church with him on Easter Sunday. Look, Jessica. I don't care how trained those soldiers were. Everybody gets tired at times. Even Navy SEALS."

"What about Jesus' post-resurrection appearances to skeptics such as James, Thomas, and Paul? And what about the five hundred witnesses? And finally, why would the disciples steal the body, yet leave the grave clothes behind? Why would any thieves take the time to carefully strip a mutilated body and lay the clothes in a pile to the side?"

Lauren started to feel a little nervous when she saw Dr. Ingraham laugh again. He held Mina in a steady gaze and said, "Young lady, you're going to be a good lawyer someday."

Scott was hoping Dr. Ingraham would provide more objections, but noticed he was actually glancing at his watch and making a move to leave. Before anyone said anything, Jessica asked, "Dr. Ingraham, *are* you going to church with Dr. Peterson? Scott and Brett have agreed to go."

"Oh, did they?" He turned to them with a puzzled look.

"Yes," Scott replied. "We agreed that if they watched part of *The Lost Tomb of Jesus* with us, we'd go to church on Easter with them."

Dr. Ingraham laughed.

Twenty-Five

EASTER SUNDAY

DR. PETERSON and Susan saved two entire rows of seats in the auditorium of the mega-church they attended. It was packed with over five thousand people. Seated with them were Dr. Ingraham and his wife and daughter, along with eight students. Scott smiled at Brett and Lauren as the guest speaker, Dr. Gary Habermas, unloaded evidence for the deity and resurrection of Jesus Christ. *I knew Dr. Peterson was up to something when he invited us all to church,* Scott thought.

After Dr. Habermas went through the Scriptures, he took a "minimum facts" approach to argue that Jesus' resurrection was physical and historical. Brett remembered hearing Jamal and Dr. Peterson adapt from this approach. This approach leverages the evidence that virtually all scholars—from liberal agnostics and skeptical atheists to fundamentalist Christians—believe about the historical Jesus. Habermas argued that regardless of theological conviction, virtually all scholars agree that the following statements about Jesus and His followers are historically true. He posted them on the giant screens:

- Jesus died by Roman crucifixion.
- He was buried, most likely in a private tomb.
- Soon afterwards the disciples were discouraged, bereaved, and despondent, having lost hope.
- Jesus' tomb was found empty very soon after His interment.[81]
- The disciples had encounters with what they believed was the risen Jesus.
- Due to these experiences, the disciples' lives were thoroughly transformed. They were even willing to die for their belief.
- The proclamation of Christ's resurrection took place very early, from the beginning of church history.
- The disciples' public testimony and preaching of the resurrection took place in the city of

Jerusalem, where Jesus had been crucified and buried shortly before.

- The earliest gospel message centered on the preaching of the death and resurrection of Jesus.
- Sunday, the day of Christ's resurrection, became the primary day for His followers to assemble and worship.
- James, the brother of Jesus and a skeptic before the resurrection, was converted because he also believed he saw the risen Jesus.
- Just a few years later, Saul of Tarsus (the apostle Paul) became a Christian after an encounter with what he believed was the risen Jesus.[82]

Near the end of his sermon of presenting a convincing argument for faith in the bodily resurrection, Dr. Habermas shared a personal story of how the resurrection of Jesus got him through the most painful experience in his own life. Habermas paused for a moment, and before the silence became a tension, he cleared his throat and continued his message.

"I'll never forget the day after Easter when I received the shocking news from my doctor, 'Your wife has stomach cancer.' That's arguably the worse kind of cancer you can get. Weeks later, I sat on my porch as Debbie was sleeping. She had a tube coming out of her stomach and I had to feed her through the tube three times a day. As Debbie slept, I sat on the porch and had my conversation with God, similar to that of Job in the Old Testament. I prayed, 'Come on, God, she's only 43 years old and she's up there dying. Lord, she is the mother of my children. She is my closest friend. Let her live.'"[83]

Susan Peterson began to tear up and looked down and saw that Jessica was also fighting back the tears.

Habermas did not get a quick response but he later felt God's comfort. It was as if He said, "Gary, I understand your hurt. I know your pain. Gary, I watched My Son die. I saw every whip lash. I watched Him asphyxiate. Do you expect better than my Son received? But Gary, I raised Him from the dead and I also will raise Debbie."

"I tried to argue God out of it, and I didn't know that in just a few days I would hold my wife's hand for the very last time. My wife was in a coma, and my sister-in-law, who is a nurse, put a stethoscope on her heart and told me to talk to her. So I told Debbie, 'I love you, I love you, I love you.' Debbie's sister told me that the most incredible thing happened. When I told Debbie that I loved her, her heart sped up. When I didn't say anything, her heart slowed down. A few minutes later, Debbie died. The date was April 9, 1995. I buried my best friend. Losing my wife was the most painful experience I've ever had to face; but if the Resurrection could help me get through her death, Christ's Resurrection can get us through anything. Heaven is living eternally with God and your loved ones. The resurrection of Jesus gives us assurance of heaven."[84]

Andrea patted Jessica's arm as they both cried. They were also thinking about their friends Nick and Jamal. But even in the midst of the pain, they were encouraged as Habermas closed with the words of Jesus in John 14, "Because I live, you also will live." They knew in a fresh way that because of the resurrection, there was hope. As Jessica heard the Christian professor end his sermon, she heard him encourage all those who had never done so to place their trust in Christ's atoning death and resurrection, and to come forward and make a profession of faith. As the choir sang a song of invitation, Jessica felt someone tap her on the shoulder. It was Lauren.

"Jessica and Andrea, will you walk down with me? I want to place my trust in Jesus."

As Dr. Peterson closed his eyes in prayer, there was great emotion going on in his spirit. His emotion, however, was interrupted by someone stepping on his foot.

"Excuse me . . . sorry, Dr. Peterson . . ."

"Oh, you're fine, Scott. Would you like me to walk down front with you?"

"I would be honored, Dr. Peterson."

As the group assembled in front—with over two hundred people making a first-time commitment to follow Jesus Christ—probably the happiest person down there that morning was Dr. Peterson, with tears streaming down his face. This time, however, Peterson was not weeping for his own sins, but for the joy of seeing some of his very own students coming to Christ. On this Easter morning, there would be no discussing or debating. Rather, these new believers would all be in agreement on the one main point. The resurrection of Jesus Christ makes all the difference!

As that special Easter day was the beginning of something new for Lauren and Scott, this very day can be the beginning of something new for you. If you have honestly faced the evidence and are willing to humble yourself and confess your faith in Jesus Christ, today can be a day of new beginning. Consider the following Scripture passages:

> Jesus told her, "I am the resurrection and the life. Anyone who believes in me will live, even after dying. Everyone who lives in me and believes in me will never ever die."[85]

> If you confess with your mouth that Jesus is Lord and believe in your heart that God raised him from the dead, you will be saved. For it is by believing in your heart

that you are made right with God, and it is by confessing with your mouth that you are saved.[86]

It is by his great mercy that we have been born again, because God raised Jesus Christ from the dead. Now we live with great expectation, and we have a priceless inheritance—an inheritance that is kept in heaven for you, pure and undefiled, beyond the reach of change and decay. And through your faith, God is protecting you by his power until you receive this salvation, which is ready to be revealed on the last day for all to see.[87]

The Coffeehouse Chronicles series includes:

Is the Bible True . . . Really?
Who Is Jesus . . . Really?
Did the Resurrection Happen . . . Really?

NOTES

1. John 15:13 NKJV
2. John 14:2–3 ESV
3. Revelation 21:3–4 ESV
4. Luke 23:43 ESV
5. 2 Corinthians 5:8
6. Luke 16:19–31 NLT
7. Luke 14:13–14
8. John 11:25–26
9. Luke 24:7
10. John 14:19
11. 1 Corinthians 15:17
12. See Romans 3:23; 5:6–11; 6:23
13. John 3:16 NKJV
14. See John 1:1–13
15. Psalm 46:1 NKJV
16. Psalm 23:4 NASB

17. 1 Thessalonians 4:13 ESV

18. Gerd Lüdemann, *What Really Happened to Jesus: A Historical Approach to the Resurrection*, trans. John Bowden (Louisville: Westminster John Knox Press, 1995), 1.

19. Acts 1:22 NASB

20. Acts 2:23–24 NASB

21. Acts 3:15 NASB, emphasis added.

22. 1 Thessalonians 1:9–10 NASB, emphasis added.

23. N. T. Wright, *The Challenge of Jesus* (Downers Grove, IL: InterVarsity Press, 1999), 220.

24. James Hastings, *Dictionary of the Apostolic Church*, vol. II (Edinburgh: T.&T. Clark, 1918), 330.

25. William Lane Craig, "Did Jesus Rise from the Dead?", as cited in Michael J. Wilkins and J. P. Moreland, *Jesus Under Fire: Modern Scholarship Reinvents the Historical Jesus* (Grand Rapids: Zondervan, 1995), 159.

26. Thomas Arnold, as cited in Wilbur Smith, *Therefore Stand: Christian Apologetics* (Grand Rapids: Baker Books, 1965), 425–26.

27. John Locke, *A Second Vindication of the Reasonableness of Christianity,* as cited in Wilbur Smith, *Therefore Stand: Christian Apologetics*, 422–23.

28. Mark 15:15–20

29. John P. Mattingly, *Crucifixion: Its Origin and Application to Christ*, unpublished Th.M. thesis, 1961, 73. Quoted by Josh McDowell, *The New Evidence That Demands a Verdict* (Nashville: Thomas Nelson, 1999), 218.

30. W. J. Sparrow-Simpson. *The Resurrection and the Christian Faith* (Grand Rapids: Zondervan, 1968), 21–22.

31. Henry Alford, *The Greek Testament: With a Critically Revised Text: A Digest of Various Readings: Marginal References to Verbal and Idiomatic Usage: Prolegomena: And a Critical and Exegetical Commentary*, vol. I. Sixth edition (Cambridge: Deighton, Bell, and Co., 1868), 298–99.

32. William D. Edwards, M.D., et al. "On the Physical Death of Jesus Christ," in *Journal of the American Medical Association* 255:11. March 21, 1986.

33. Samuel Houghton, as cited in Frederick Charles Cook, ed. *Commentary on the Holy Bible* (London: John Murray, 1878), 349–50.

34. Ibid.

35. Isaiah 53:2–12

36. Isaiah 53:8–9

37. Craig, "Did Jesus Rise from the Dead?", as cited in Wilkins and Moreland, *Jesus Under Fire*, 148–49.

38. Ibid.

39. Alfred Edersheim, *The Life and Times of Jesus the Messiah*, vol. II. (Grand Rapids: Eerdmans, 1962), 617.

40. Wilbur M. Smith, *Therefore Stand: Christian Apologetics*, 370–71.

41. Norman L. Geisler and Frank Turek, *I Don't Have Enough Faith to Be an Atheist* (Wheaton: Crossway, 2004), 275.

42. William Smith, *Dictionary of Greek and Roman Antiquities*, rev. ed. (London: James Walton and John Murray, 1870), 250–51.

43. Matthew 27:62–66 NKJV

44. A. T. Robertson, *Word Pictures in the New Testament.* 5 vols. (Nashville: Broadman Press, 1930). Reprint (New York: R.R. Smith, Inc., 1931), 239.

45. Ibid.

46. Alfred Edersheim, *The Temple: Its Ministry and Services* (Grand Rapids: Eerdmans, 1958), 147–49.

47. The Mishnah, trans. Herbert Danby (London: Geoffrey Cumberlege, Oxford Press, 1933), 1.2.

48. Mark 14:50

49. J. P. Moreland, *Scaling the Secular City* (Grand Rapids: Baker Books, 1987), 168.

50. Matthew 28:2–4 NKJV

51. Matthew 28:11–15 NKJV

52. Albert Roper, *Did Jesus Rise from the Dead?* (Grand Rapids: Zondervan, 1965), 33.

53. T. G. Tucker, *Life in the Roman World of Nero and St. Paul* (New York: Macmillan Company, 1910), 342–44.

54. Thomas Thorburn, *The Resurrection Narratives and Modern Criticisms* (London: Kegan, Trench, Trubner & Co., Ltd., 1910), 179–82.

55. J. N. D. Anderson, "The Resurrection of Jesus Christ" in *Christianity Today* (March 29, 1968), 4–9.

56. Norman Anderson, *Christianity and World Religions*, rev. ed. *Of Christianity and Comparative Religions* (Downers Grove, IL: InterVarsity Press, 1984), 95–96.

57. Moreland, *Scaling the Secular City*, 168.

58. John Warwick Montgomery, *History and Christianity* (Downers Grove, IL: InterVarsity Press, 1964), 78.

59. Craig, "Did Jesus Rise from the Dead?", as cited in Wilkins and Moreland, *Jesus Under Fire*, 157.

60. Ibid.

61. Acts 25:6–7

62. Acts 25:19 NKJV

63. Acts 17:32 NKJV

64. Acts 26:23

65. Acts 26:24–28

66. The Discovery Channel, http://dsc.discovery.com/convergence/tomb/about/about.html

67. http://www.garyhabermas.com/articles/The_Lost_Tomb_of_Jesus/losttombofjesus_response.htm

68. Ibid.

69. Ibid.

70. Kirsopp Lake, *The Historical Evidence for the Resurrection of Jesus Christ* (New York: Putnam's Sons, 1907).

71. William Lane Craig, *The Son Rises* (Eugene: Wipf and Stock Publishers, 2000), 42.

72. Gary R. Habermas, *The Verdict of History* (Nashville: Thomas Nelson, 1988), 119.

73. Theodore R. Sarbin and Joseph B. Juhasz, "The Social Contract of Hallucinations," Hallucinations: Behaviour, Experience and Theory, edited by R. K. Siegel and L. J. West (New York: John Wiley & Sons, 1975), 242.

74. Gary Collins, PhD, in personal correspondence, recorded in Gary R. Habermas, "The Recent Revival of Hallucination Theories," in *Christian Research Journal*, vol. 23, no. 4 (August 13, 2001), 48.

75. Ibid.

76. Mark 12:1–12; especially verse 12

77. Adapted from Michael Licona, *Paul Meets Muhammad: A Christian-Muslim Debate on the Resurrection* (Grand Rapids: Baker Books, 2006), 55.

78. See Matthew 28:11–15

79. Justin Martyr, Dialogue Against Trypho #108.

80. Charles Colson, *How Now Shall We Live?* (Wheaton: Tyndale, 1999), 275–76.

81. This is the only point that does not meet the criteria of "minimum facts." Nevertheless, Habermas reports that nearly seventy-five percent of scholars on the subject accept the empty tomb as a historical fact.

82. Gary Habermas, *The Risen Jesus and Future Hope* (Lanham, MD: Rowman & Littlefield, 2003), 9–10, quoted by Geisler and Turek, *I Don't Have Enough Faith to Be an Atheist*, 299–300.

83. Dr. Habermas's testimony adapted from several podcast testimonies on www.garyhabermas.com

84. Ibid.

85. John 11:25–26 NLT

86. Romans 10:9–10 NLT

87. 1 Peter 1:3–5 NLT

ACKNOWLEDGMENTS

WE WOULD LIKE to thank Randall Payleitner, our acquisitions editor at Moody Publishers, for his extensive work and outstanding services to help make this book possible. Also, we thank Paul Santhouse for his excellent editing, and Clay Sterrett (Dave's father) for reading the initial manuscript and providing feedback, corrections, and encouragement.

The authors are grateful for permission to use the following copyrighted material:

Excerpts from *More Than a Carpenter*, by Josh McDowell and Sean McDowell, © 2009 by Josh McDowell and Sean McDowell. Used by permission of Tyndale House Publishers.

 Excerpts from *The New Evidence That Demands a Verdict*, by Josh McDowell, ©1999 by Josh McDowell. Used by permission of Thomas Nelson Publishers.

The Coffee House Chronicles

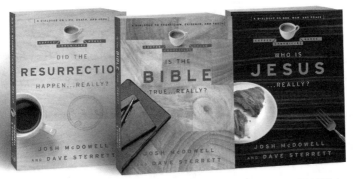

ISBN-13: 978-0-8024-8768-1

ISBN-13: 978-0-8024-8766-7

ISBN-13: 978-0-8024-8767-4

With over 40 million books sold, bestselling author Josh McDowell is no stranger to creatively presenting biblical truth. Now, partnering with fellow apologist Dave Sterrett, Josh introduces a new series targeted at the intersection of story and truth.

The Coffee House Chronicles are short, easily devoured novellas aimed at answering prevalent spiritual questions. Each book in the series tackles a long-contested question of the faith, and then answers these questions with truth through relationships and dialogue in each story.

MOODY
PUBLISHERS

www.MoodyPublishers.com

Why Trust Jesus?

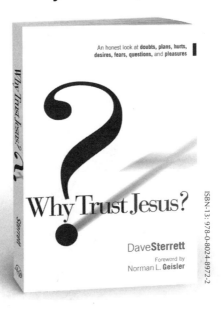

Our generation is up for grabs! Our trust has been shattered in other areas as we have seen hypocrisy in governmental leaders as well as in the church. We are looking for relationships that are authentic and full of life, but we have many questions in regard to faith, reason, suffering and even the person of Jesus himself.

MOODY
PUBLISHERS

www.MoodyPublishers.com

Just Do Something

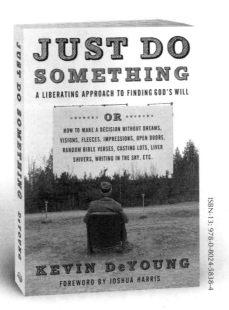

Hyperspiritual approaches to finding God's will just don't work. It's time to try something new: give up. God doesn't need to tell us what to do at each fork in the road. He's already revealed His plan for our lives: to love Him with our whole hearts, to obey His Word, and after that, to do what we like. No need for hocus-pocus. No reason to be directionally challenged. *Just Do Something.*

MOODY
PUBLISHERS

www.MoodyPublishers.com

READ THE STORY.

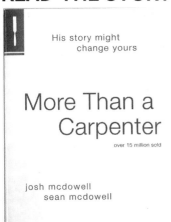

His story might
change yours

More Than a Carpenter

over 15 million sold

josh mcdowell
sean mcdowell

Available in 6-pack or 30-pack sets for best value.

Since its original publication in 1977, this modern classic has over 15 million copies in print and has introduced countless people to Jesus. Now, in this newly updated version, Josh and his son Sean reexamine the evidence for today's generation: Is Jesus really the Lord he claimed to be?

WEIGH THE FACTS.

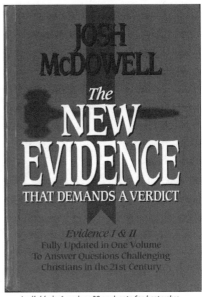

Maintaining its classic defense of the faith, this fully updated volume provides a wealth of historical, archaeological, and bibliographical evidences for the basic tenets of Christian belief.

Available in 6-pack or 30-pack sets for best value.

ORDER YOURS TODAY!
Visit www.josh.org/store or your favorite bookseller.